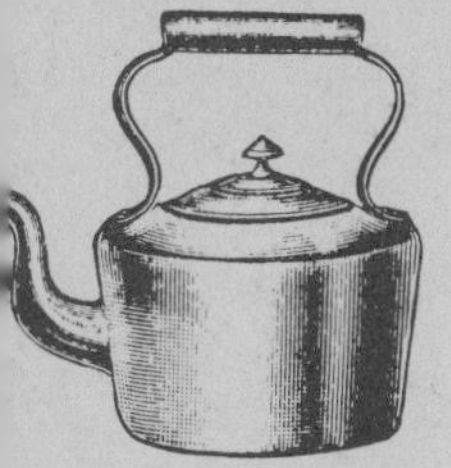

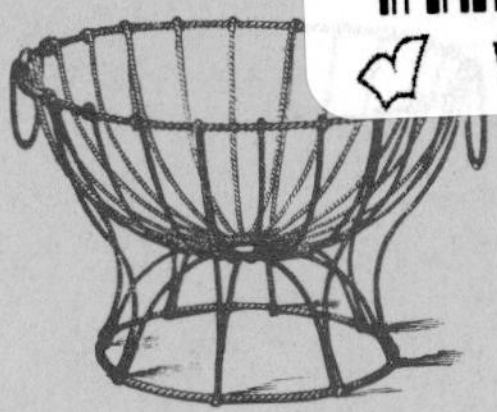

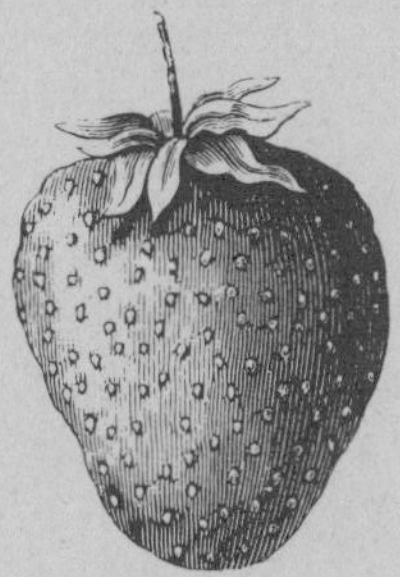

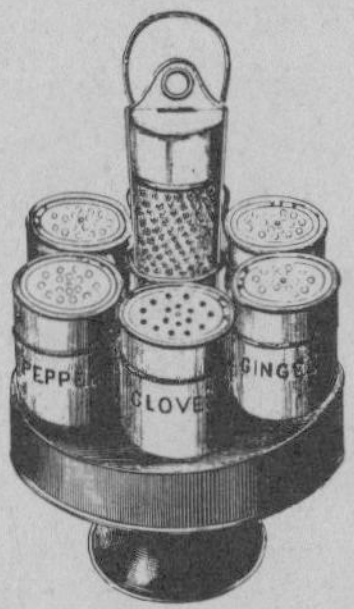
CLOVES

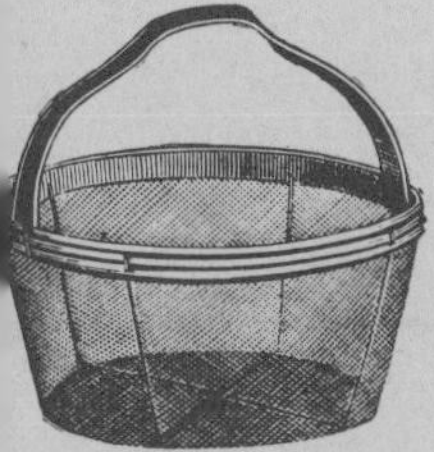

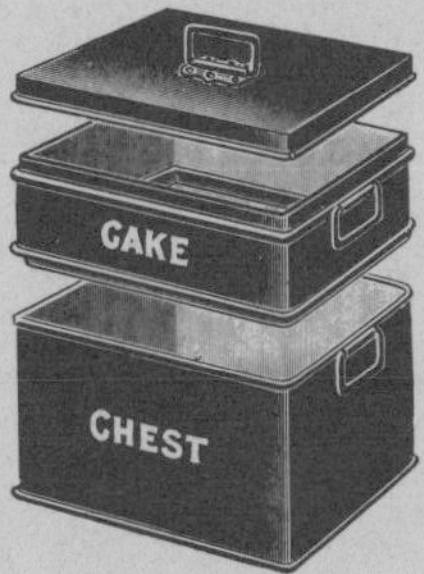
CAKE
CHEST

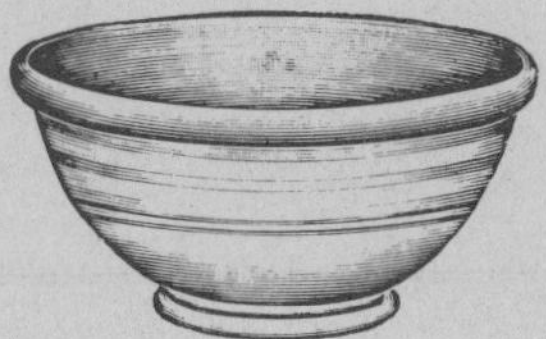

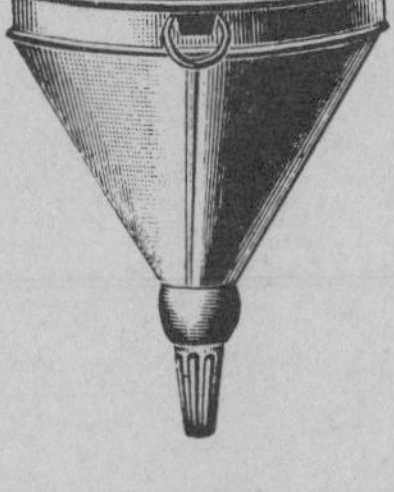

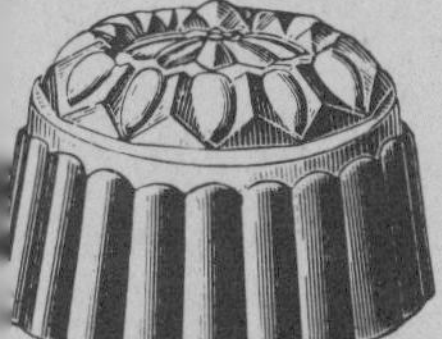

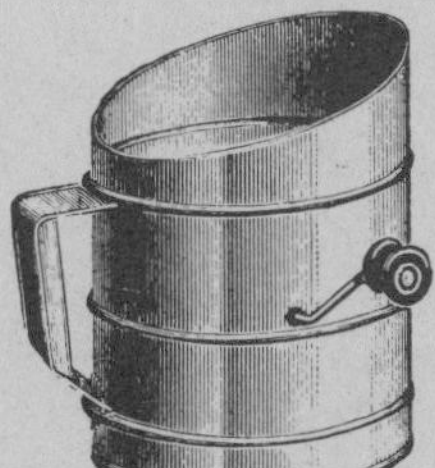

Southern Living

The
SOUTHERN
HERITAGE
COOKBOOK
LIBRARY

The SOUTHERN HERITAGE
Socials
and
Soirées
COOKBOOK

OXMOOR HOUSE
Birmingham, Alabama

Southern Living ®

The Southern Heritage Cookbook Library

Copyright 1985 by Oxmoor House, Inc.
Book Division of Southern Progress Corporation
P.O. Box 2463, Birmingham, Alabama 35201

Southern Living® is a federally registered trademark belonging to Southern Living, Inc.

Library of Congress Catalog Number: 85-060121
ISBN: 0-8487-0617-X

Manufactured in the United States of America

The Southern Heritage SOCIALS AND SOIREES Cookbook

Executive Editor: Ann H. Harvey
Southern Living® *Foods Editor:* Jean W. Liles
Senior Editor: Joan E. Denman
Senior Foods Editor: Katherine M. Eakin
Assistant Editor: Ellen de Lathouder
Assistant Foods Editor: Helen R. Turk
Director, Test Kitchen: Laura N. Massey
Test Kitchen Home Economists: Kay E. Clarke, Rebecca J. Riddle, Elizabeth J. Taliaferro, Dee Waller, Elise Wright Walker
Production Manager: Jerry R. Higdon
Copy Editor: Melinda E. West
Editorial Assistants: Mary Ann Laurens, Karen P. Traccarella
Food Photographer: Jim Bathie
Food Stylist: Sara Jane Ball
Layout Designer: Christian von Rosenvinge
Mechanical Artist: Faith Nance
Research Editors: Alicia Hathaway, Philip Napoli

Special Consultants

Art Director: Irwin Glusker
Heritage Consultant: Meryle Evans
Foods Writer: Lillian B. Marshall
Food and Recipe Consultants: Marilyn Wyrick Ingram, Audrey P. Stehle

Cover: The Victorian Tea menu (page 67) is pictured in all its delicious splendor.

Collection of Bonnie Slotnick

CONTENTS

INTRODUCTION

Through good times and rock-bottom misery, the South has never forgotten how to play. It is this propensity for making the best of things that has always colored the way the Southerner views his fun times. A lady of post-Civil War Atlanta never let poverty stand in the way of inviting friends in to share a pot of tea, and by the same token, when a young man from Savannah came into wealth, the first thing he thought about was putting on a ball for his friends. In those days, it was not unheard of for a host to hire servants from neighboring plantations in order to provide a ratio of one waiter per guest.

Historically, then, we are party people. Like it or no, we inherited a reputation for openhandedness with our food and drink and open-mindedness about gaming and dancing. Just name a time of day; we will produce a suitable menu as quickly as one can compose a guest list.

Now it is quite possible that not everyone aspires to giving a great ball and entertainment or a "Drawing Room" à la Dolley Madison, at least not frequently. Accounts of the outlandishly extravagant parties Rebecca (Bettie) Brown of Galveston and other people of wealth and position were used to are included here for leavening and illustration. To reproduce a Bettie Brown fantasia today, it would be necessary to hire a medium-sized museum, not to mention the necessity for appropriate clothes and jewels.

There have been occasions for women only, as witness the old-fashioned quilting bee, which, incidentally, is enjoying a resurgence. There still are projects that have a more direct bearing upon women than men. The League of Women Voters and the Older Women's League are examples. Woman's clubs and garden clubs still have their motivation rooted in public betterment. Historic homes and monuments? In these matters women have traditionally taken the lead.

People with unlimited means have ever been objects of awe for the splendor of their parties. Dolley Madison was a bright star in that firmament. And we have a history of balls sponsored by the likes of the 1800s german clubs, the Naval Academy at Annapolis, and the celebrations for George Washington and Andrew Jackson that really are more than just fun reading. These memories will work for us today if we are open to them; they contain the elements of style.

FOR MORNING CALL

T he coffee as a morning party has become one of the hallmarks of Southern hospitality. Certainly there was an upswing in coffee drinking as a result of the colonists' anti-tea declarations preceding the Revolutionary War, but it was in the South, more than elsewhere, that women had the leisure to include morning entertainments. Too, Southern women remained in the home for a number of years after their Northern counterparts entered the outside working world.

A coffee can be a spur-of-the-moment idea, as when neighbors are out planting petunias or separating tulip bulbs, or when the rising sweet rolls in the kitchen call time out for a coffee. But there are more serious times when nothing fits the exigencies of a social situation but a bona fide coffee. Let's say a number of people are vying for a chance to entertain for an out-of-towner, a bride, a celebrity, or a political figure, and that person's time is overcommitted. Or perhaps it is simply a crowded holiday docket. What does the determined hostess do? She declares a coffee. It may take place anytime between ten and noon, and there is a wide latitude in the foods which may appropriately be served. The arrangements may be formal or casual. The number of guests is limited only by the physical setup.

It is perhaps this extreme flexibility, the "anything-goes" feeling, that makes the coffee such a valuable entertainment art form. It would be rare today, however, to see a morning party as elaborate as the ones in this chapter given by Rebecca Ashton Brown or the ladies of the Nashville Centennial Club. Along with those days, also past are the thrilling newspaper descriptions of the floral arrangements present in each room: "In the gold drawing room Easter lilies were arranged." Also given their due were the attending ladies' exquisite gowns: "White crepe cashmere satin" or "white mull, figured in blue rosebuds."

Youngsters have morning rallies too, but not with coffee. Theirs is a *Coca-Cola* party with good things to eat. And, just as we offer coffee at a tea and tea at a coffee, they choose among soft drinks, punch, and iced tea.

Mocha Punch and coffee, tailored for morning call. Clockwise from left: Tomato-Egg Sandwiches, Cheese-Bacon Puffs, Swedish Rose Cookies, Amandine Chicken Sandwiches, and Coffee Cake Squares.

This Atlanta coffee reflects the Southern art of fashionable leisure, c.1900.

MORNING COFFEE IN ATLANTA

A coffee may be the early bird's tea party and, like the tea, may be as casual or as dressy as the hostess wants it to be. In Atlanta, where cooking for company comes as naturally as breathing, the optimum number of guests for coffee is from six to twenty-six. Dainty open-faced sandwiches come with a cup of fresh brewed coffee, and there's always the Southern essential: irresistible diet-defying sweets. Making party sandwiches ahead? Frozen bread cuts and spreads better than soft. Butter is better than mayonnaise when sandwiches are to be frozen. For overnight, wrap in a damp towel and cover with aluminum foil; refrigerate.

AMANDINE CHICKEN SANDWICHES
TOMATO-EGG SANDWICHES
CHEESE-BACON PUFFS
LEMON TRIANGLES
COFFEE CAKE SQUARES
SWEDISH ROSE COOKIES
PASTEL MINTS
FROSTY MOCHA PUNCH
HOT COFFEE

Serves 10 to 12

AMANDINE CHICKEN SANDWICHES

1 cup ground cooked
   chicken
¼ cup blanched almonds,
   chopped
¾ cup mayonnaise
Dash of salt
Dash of pepper
Dash of curry powder
18 slices whole wheat bread
Pimiento strips

Combine first 6 ingredients in a small mixing bowl; stir until well blended. Cover and chill.

Cut bread into rounds, using a 2-inch biscuit cutter. Cut each round in half. Spread half-rounds with chicken mixture; garnish with pimiento strips. Cover and chill. Yield: 3 dozen.

TOMATO-EGG SANDWICHES

12 slices rye bread
1 cup mayonnaise
4 hard-cooked eggs, sliced
8 cherry tomatoes, sliced
Fresh parsley sprigs

Cut bread into 24 rounds, using a 2-inch biscuit cutter. Spread each round with a small amount of mayonnaise. Spoon remaining mayonnaise into a pastry bag fitted with a small star tip; set aside.

Top bread rounds with a slice each of hard-cooked egg and cherry tomato. Pipe reserved mayonnaise on tops, and garnish each with fresh parsley. Cover and chill. Yield: 2 dozen.

CHEESE-BACON PUFFS

9 slices white bread
3 eggs, well beaten
1½ cups (6 ounces) shredded
   sharp Cheddar cheese
1 tablespoon grated onion
¾ teaspoon dry mustard
9 slices bacon, cooked and
   crumbled

Remove crust from bread. Cut each slice into 4 squares, and place on ungreased baking sheets.

Combine eggs, cheese, onion, and mustard in a medium mixing bowl; stir well.

Place 1 teaspoon cheese mixture on each bread square. Sprinkle with bacon.

Bake at 375° for 15 minutes or until cheese mixture is slightly puffed. Serve warm. Yield: 3 dozen.

A New Orleans coffee label, 1910. Woman's Club brand implied good taste.

LEMON TRIANGLES

1 cup raisins
½ cup coarsely chopped
   pecans
Grated rind of 1 lemon
1 cup mayonnaise
1 cup sugar
1 egg
16 slices toast,
   crust removed

Grind together raisins, pecans, and lemon rind in a small mixing bowl, using fine blade of a meat grinder or steel chopping blade of a food processor. Set aside.

Combine mayonnaise, sugar, and egg in a medium saucepan; place over medium-low heat. Cook, stirring constantly, 10 minutes or until slightly thickened. Remove from heat, and fold in reserved fruit mixture.

Cut each slice of toast into 4 triangles. Spread 1 heaping teaspoon fruit mixture on each triangle. Serve immediately. Yield: about 5 dozen.

THREE POUNDS.   NET WEIGHT.

WOMAN'S CLUB

BRAND

COFFEE

New Orleans Packing Co., Inc.,
NEW ORLEANS.

Frosty Mocha Punch is a cool counterpoint to the requisite hot coffee at morning parties.

PASTEL MINTS

½ cup butter, softened
1 (16-ounce) package powdered sugar, sifted
2 tablespoons evaporated milk
¼ teaspoon peppermint oil
2 drops of desired food coloring

Cream butter in a large mixing bowl; add remaining ingredients, mixing well. Knead in bowl until mixture is smooth.

Shape mint mixture into long ropes, ½ inch in diameter. Place ropes on ungreased baking sheets; cut each rope into 1-inch pieces.

Cover and let stand overnight to dry. Store in airtight containers. Yield: about 20 dozen.

COFFEE CAKE SQUARES

½ cup butter or margarine, softened
1¼ cups sugar, divided
2 eggs
1 (8-ounce) carton commercial sour cream
¾ teaspoon baking soda
1½ cups all-purpose flour
1½ teaspoons baking powder
1 teaspoon vanilla extract
¾ cup chopped walnuts
1 tablespoon ground cinnamon

Cream butter in a large mixing bowl; gradually add 1 cup sugar, beating well. Add eggs, beating well. Combine sour cream and soda; add to creamed mixture, beating well.

Combine flour and baking powder in a small mixing bowl; stir well. Add flour mixture and vanilla to creamed mixture, beating well. Pour half of batter into a greased 13- x 9- x 2-inch baking pan.

Combine remaining sugar, walnuts, and cinnamon; sprinkle half of mixture over batter. Spoon remaining batter over nut mixture; sprinkle with remaining nut mixture.

Bake at 350° for 25 minutes or until a wooden pick inserted in center comes out clean. Cut into 1½-inch squares. Serve warm. Yield: about 4 dozen.

SWEDISH ROSE COOKIES

1½ cups butter, softened
¾ cup sugar
4 cups all-purpose flour
¼ cup plus 2 tablespoons strawberry jam

Cream butter; gradually add sugar, beating until light and fluffy. Add flour; stir well. Cover and chill 1 hour.

Shape dough into 1-inch balls, and place 2 inches apart on ungreased cookie sheets. Press thumb into balls; fill with ¼ teaspoon strawberry jam.

Bake at 375° for 12 minutes. Cool slightly on cookie sheets; remove to wire racks. Yield: 6 dozen.

FROSTY MOCHA PUNCH

2 quarts strong brewed coffee
¼ cup sugar
3 tablespoons vanilla extract
½ gallon coffee ice cream, softened
3 cups whipping cream, whipped
Additional whipped cream (optional)

Combine coffee and sugar in a large mixing bowl, stirring until sugar dissolves. Stir in vanilla; chill thoroughly.

Spoon ice cream and 3 cups whipped cream into punch bowl. Slowly pour chilled coffee mixture into punch bowl; stir to blend. Dollop additional whipped cream on top, if desired. Yield: about 1 gallon.

RECIPE SWAP COFFEE

G ood fences make good neighbors"? Not so, they say down in Jackson, Mississippi. Good cooks make good neighbors. Longtime residents of one historic street have passed so many recipes over their fences and attended so many recipe swapping parties that they have accumulated priceless files to which they turn even more frequently than to their cookbooks. "This is Mrs. So-and-So's Fig Preserves Cake," or "Mrs. So-and-So brought a basket of these hot rolls and the recipe the day we moved in eight years ago." Sometimes a group gets together to share a find from a magazine or a recipe enclosed in a letter from afar. Could there be a better way to remember a friend? Women today might even declare a coffee to swap coupons instead of recipes. Whatever the swap — a coffee may be as productive as it is fun.

RAISIN BISCUITS
LEMON MARMALADE
CHOCOLATE PINWHEEL COOKIES
FIG PRESERVES CAKE
COFFEE

Serves 8

On front side of "Turn Card" neighbors share a windowsill visit, c.1890.

A COMPROMISE.

He: "Seal Brand Coffee leads the rest"
She: "Royal Gem Tea Brand is best"
He: "Still we need not disagree."
Mine's best coffee; your's best tea"
She: "thus to fix it I'm not loath
Since Chase and Sanborn import them both".

The windowsill visit includes an exchange of favorite beverages.

RAISIN BISCUITS

2 cups all-purpose
   flour
1 tablespoon plus 1 teaspoon
   baking powder
1 teaspoon salt
¼ cup plus 2 tablespoons
   shortening
½ cup raisins
¾ cup milk
Melted butter

Sift together flour, baking powder, and salt in a medium mixing bowl; cut in shortening with a pastry blender until mixture resembles coarse meal. Stir in raisins. Sprinkle milk evenly over flour mixture, stirring with a fork just until dry ingredients are moistened.

Turn dough out onto a lightly floured surface; pat to ½-inch thickness. Cut dough with a 2-inch biscuit cutter. Place biscuits on lightly greased baking sheets, and brush tops with melted butter. Bake at 450° for 10 minutes or until lightly browned. Serve warm with Lemon Marmalade. Yield: about 1½ dozen.

LEMON MARMALADE

12 lemons (about 2 pounds)
1 quart water
4 cups sugar

Cut lemons in thin slices; remove seeds. Place seeds in a cheesecloth bag. Tie bag securely, and set aside. Combine lemon slices and water in a shallow dish. Cover and let stand at room temperature overnight.

Transfer lemon mixture to a large Dutch oven; bring to a boil. Boil gently 30 minutes or until mixture is reduced to 1 quart. Stir in sugar, and add reserved cheesecloth bag of seeds; return to a boil, and cook rapidly 15 minutes or until mixture sheets off a metal spoon. As mixture begins to thicken, stir frequently to prevent sticking. Remove from heat; remove and discard cheesecloth bag.

Quickly ladle marmalade into hot, sterilized jars, leaving ¼-inch headspace; cover at once with metal lids, and screw bands tight. Process in boiling-water bath 15 minutes. Yield: 5 half-pints.

Just when coffee emerged as a beverage may never be known, but by the fourteenth century, coffee was being used as a morning beverage in the Middle East. The word derives from the Arabic, but most experts agree that coffee had its origin in Ethiopia. It is now grown in many parts of the world. As early as six years before the Boston Tea Party in America, tea was becoming too political to be drinkable. When the housewives of Falmouth, Massachusetts, switched from tea to coffee, even John Adams followed suit. America's affair with the cup of coffee, which readily adapted to morning socials, had begun. All that remained to be found was a good biscuit and some marmalade.

CHOCOLATE PINWHEEL COOKIES

½ cup shortening
½ cup sugar
1 egg yolk, lightly beaten
3 tablespoons milk
1½ teaspoons vanilla
  extract
1½ cups all-purpose flour
1 teaspoon baking powder
⅛ teaspoon salt
1 (1-ounce) square
  unsweetened chocolate,
  melted

Cream shortening in a large mixing bowl; gradually add sugar, beating until light and fluffy. Add egg yolk and milk; mix well. Stir in vanilla.

Sift together flour, baking powder, and salt; gradually add to creamed mixture, stirring well. Divide dough in half; add melted chocolate to one half of dough, mixing until well blended. Cover and chill at least 1 hour.

Place chocolate dough between two pieces of waxed paper. Roll into an 8- x 6-inch rectangle. Repeat rolling procedure with plain dough. Remove top sheets of waxed paper, and place plain dough on top of chocolate dough. Starting at long end, lift dough from waxed paper, and roll up jellyroll fashion. Wrap in waxed paper, and chill several hours.

Cut dough into ¼-inch-thick slices, and place 1 inch apart on lightly greased cookie sheets. Bake at 350° for 8 to 10 minutes. Cool 1 minute on cookie sheets; remove to wire racks to cool completely. Yield: about 2½ dozen.

Serve as many goodies as you please with coffee, but some folks only want Fig Preserves Cake.

FIG PRESERVES CAKE

1 teaspoon baking soda
1 cup buttermilk
2 cups all-purpose flour
1½ cups sugar
1 teaspoon salt
1½ teaspoons ground
  cinnamon
1 teaspoon ground nutmeg
1 teaspoon ground cloves
1 cup vegetable oil
3 eggs
1 cup fig preserves
1 teaspoon vanilla extract
2 cups chopped pecans
Glaze (recipe follows)

Dissolve soda in buttermilk; set aside.

Sift together flour, sugar, salt, cinnamon, nutmeg, and cloves in a large bowl; add oil, beating well. Add eggs, one at a time, mixing well after each addition. Stir in reserved buttermilk mixture, fig preserves, vanilla, and pecans; mix well.

Pour batter into a greased 10-inch tube pan. Bake at 350° for 1 hour and 15 minutes or until a wooden pick inserted in center comes out clean. Cool in pan 10 minutes, and remove from pan. Pierce cake several times with a long fork. Slowly pour glaze over cake; cool completely. Yield: one 10-inch cake.

Glaze:

1 cup sugar
½ cup buttermilk
½ cup butter or margarine
1 teaspoon light corn syrup
½ teaspoon salt

Combine all ingredients in a medium saucepan. Cook over medium heat, stirring frequently, until mixture comes to a boil. Boil 3 minutes, stirring constantly. Remove from heat; cool slightly. Yield: glaze for one 10-inch cake.

VICKSBURG COCA-COLA® PARTY

The serendipitous *Coca-Cola* party, so beloved by the young, could never have come into being without the inspiration of an Atlanta druggist, John S. Pemberton. In 1886, with no thought of giving pleasure, he combined coca leaves and kola nuts to make a remedy for hangovers and headaches in general. He called it coca-cola. Another Atlanta druggist bought Pemberton out for $2,000. The secret formula was sold and resold. The beverage's real growth began under the leadership of Asa G. Candler, a native of Villa Rica, Georgia. By 1891 he owned the formula outright. Vicksburg, Mississippi, home of the first commercial bottling plant, takes pride in its Coca-Cola Museum. Here's our not-so-secret formula for a party that's sure to please.

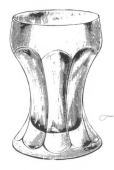

CREAM CHEESE DIP
CRAB SALAD SANDWICHES
ANNE'S PIMIENTO CHEESE SANDWICHES
DEVILED HAM PUFFS
TORTE BARS
BUTTER TOASTED PECANS
BLACK COWS
COLAS

Serves 16

CREAM CHEESE DIP

2 (8-ounce) packages cream cheese, softened
½ cup plus 2 tablespoons mayonnaise
¼ cup minced fresh parsley
2 teaspoons grated onion
1 teaspoon Worcestershire sauce
¼ teaspoon salt
¼ teaspoon red pepper

Combine all ingredients in a large mixing bowl; beat at medium speed of an electric mixer until well blended. Cover and chill thoroughly.

Spoon dip into a serving container, and serve with chips or fresh vegetables. Yield: about 2½ cups.

CRAB SALAD SANDWICHES

1 cup flake crabmeat, drained
½ cup mayonnaise
4 stalks celery, finely chopped
2 hard-cooked eggs, chopped
1 tablespoon chopped pimiento
½ teaspoon salt
¼ teaspoon pepper
21 slices white bread
Sliced pimiento-stuffed olives

Combine crabmeat, mayonnaise, celery, egg, pimiento, salt, and pepper in a medium mixing bowl; mix well. Cover and chill thoroughly.

Cut 2 rounds from each bread slice, using a 1¾-inch biscuit cutter. Spread 1 teaspoon mixture evenly on 21 rounds; top with remaining bread rounds. Place an olive slice on top of each sandwich; secure with a wooden pick. Cover and refrigerate until ready to serve. Yield: 24 appetizer sandwiches.

ANNE'S PIMIENTO CHEESE SANDWICHES

1 whole pimiento
3 cups (12 ounces) finely shredded extra sharp Cheddar cheese
⅓ cup mayonnaise
2 teaspoons finely grated onion
1 teaspoon lemon juice
⅛ to ¼ teaspoon red pepper
24 slices bread

Mash pimiento in a large mixing bowl, using a fork. Add remaining ingredients, except bread, and mix until well blended.

Spread pimiento cheese mixture evenly over 12 bread slices. Top with remaining bread slices; remove crust, and slice sandwiches in half. Serve immediately. Yield: 2 dozen.

Black Cows are a wonderful concoction. Here served with Deviled Ham Puffs and Anne's Pimiento Cheese Sandwiches.

The "Dinner at Eight" camera paused for another camera to shoot this Coca-Cola ad on the Hollywood set in 1933. Standing in center are Lionel Barrymore and Jean Harlow.

DEVILED HAM PUFFS

1 (8-ounce) package cream cheese, softened
1 egg yolk, beaten
1 teaspoon onion juice
½ teaspoon baking powder
¼ teaspoon salt
¼ teaspoon prepared horseradish
¼ teaspoon hot sauce
16 slices bread
3 (2¼-ounce) cans deviled ham
Sliced pimiento-stuffed olives

Combine first 7 ingredients in a medium mixing bowl. Beat at medium speed of an electric mixer until blended. Set aside.

Cut 2 rounds from each bread slice, using a 2-inch biscuit cutter. Toast bread rounds on one side. Spread untoasted side evenly with deviled ham, and place on ungreased baking sheets. Top each with 1 heaping teaspoon reserved cheese mixture; spread evenly over deviled ham. Bake at 375° for 10 minutes or until puffed and lightly browned. Garnish with olive slices. Serve immediately. Yield: about 2½ dozen.

TORTE BARS

3 cups all-purpose flour
2 teaspoons baking powder
½ teaspoon salt
1 cup butter or margarine, softened
2 cups sugar
4 eggs, beaten
2½ teaspoons vanilla extract, divided
1 cup chopped pecans
2 egg whites
1½ cups firmly packed light brown sugar

Sift together flour, baking powder, and salt in a medium mixing bowl; set aside.

Cream butter in a large mixing bowl; gradually add 2 cups sugar, beating well. Add beaten eggs and 1½ teaspoons vanilla, mixing well. Stir in flour mixture and pecans. Spoon batter evenly into 2 greased 13- x 9- x 2-inch baking pans.

Beat 2 egg whites (at room temperature) until stiff peaks form; gradually add brown sugar, 2 tablespoons at a time, beating well after each addition. Fold in remaining vanilla. Spread evenly over batter in baking pans.

Bake at 350° for 30 minutes. Cool completely in pans. Cut into 3- x 1½-inch bars to serve. Yield: about 4 dozen.

BUTTER TOASTED PECANS

1½ pounds pecan halves, divided
¾ cup butter or margarine, melted and divided
1½ teaspoons salt, divided

Spread half of pecans in a 15-x 10- x 1-inch jellyroll pan. Drizzle half of butter over pecans; stir well. Sprinkle pecans with ¾ teaspoon salt, stirring well.

Bake at 325° for 18 to 20 minutes, stirring pecans at 5 minute intervals. Cool completely in pan. Repeat procedure with remaining ingredients. Store in airtight containers. Yield: 16 servings.

BLACK COWS

1 gallon vanilla ice cream
10 (10-ounce) bottles cola, chilled

Place 2 scoops ice cream in each of sixteen 10-ounce glasses. Pour cola over ice cream. Yield: 16 servings.

On May 1, 1889, an ad appeared in the *Atlanta Journal* announcing Asa G. Candler and Company as proprietor of *Coca-Cola.* "Delicious/Refreshing/Exhilarating" defined the qualities of a soft drink that was to launch one of the most successful companies in the world. Undeniably, the home-cultivated character of Asa Candler was the real formula for success. From his farmer-merchant father, he acquired the virtue of hard, honest labor and from his resolute mother, a sense of cultural and spiritual responsibility — the best values Southern tradition can endow.

Colas add to the fun at a Georgia house party, 1913.

Georgia Department of Archives and History

MORGING CALL

Galveston pulled out all the stops when the Texas State Lumbermen's Association came to town around the turn of the century. The visiting wives were feted royally by society and its leading light, Rebecca (Bettie) Ashton Brown. Unconventional Bettie was equally as comfortable wearing her $5,000 lace coat to a garden party as she was standing atop a ladder directing a crew of workmen. The visiting ladies were treated to a boat ride on the bay, an auto ride over the city, an oyster roast, and a ball. But they remembered most vividly their morning call at Ashton Villa and Bettie's collation of sandwiches, chocolate, confections, and tea.

VEGETABLE SANDWICHES
PRINCESS SANDWICHES
OLIVE-CHEESE SANDWICHES
ALMOND MERINGUE COOKIES
CHOCOLATE-MOCHA CHEESECAKES
STUFFED DRIED FRUIT
TEA

Serves 12

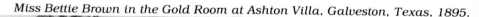

Miss Bettie Brown in the Gold Room at Ashton Villa, Galveston, Texas, 1895.

A stroll along Galveston's Avenue I, photographed five years before the devastating hurricane of 1900.

VEGETABLE SANDWICHES

1 tomato, peeled and finely
   chopped
1 small cucumber, peeled,
   seeded, and finely chopped
1 small green pepper, seeded
   and finely chopped
1 small onion, finely chopped
½ cup finely chopped celery
½ envelope unflavored gelatin
2 tablespoons vegetable juice
   cocktail
1 cup mayonnaise
Dash of salt
64 slices thin-sliced white
   bread, crust removed

Combine tomato, cucumber, green pepper, onion, and celery in a large colander to drain; set aside.

Combine gelatin and vegetable juice cocktail in a small saucepan. Cook over low heat, stirring constantly, until gelatin dissolves. Remove from heat.

Combine gelatin mixture, mayonnaise, and salt in a large mixing bowl; stir until well blended. Fold in reserved vegetables. Cover and refrigerate overnight.

Stir mixture well, and spread 1 heaping tablespoon on 32 bread slices; top with remaining bread slices. Cut each sandwich in half lengthwise. Serve immediately. Yield: about 5 dozen.

Note: Vegetable mixture may be refrigerated up to 4 days and sandwiches assembled as needed.

PRINCESS SANDWICHES

½ cup ground, cooked
   chicken
½ cup ground, cooked ham
½ cup (2 ounces) shredded
   sharp Cheddar cheese
2 hard-cooked eggs, finely
   chopped
3 tablespoons salad
   dressing
1 teaspoon vinegar
¼ teaspoon salt
Dash of pepper
¼ cup butter or margarine,
   softened
12 slices thin-sliced white
   bread, crust removed
12 slices thin-sliced whole
   wheat bread, crust removed

Combine chicken, ham, cheese, egg, salad dressing, vinegar, salt, and pepper in a small mixing bowl; stir until well blended. Cover and chill.

Spread softened butter evenly over bread slices. Spread 1 heaping tablespoon meat-cheese mixture over each slice of white bread; top with a slice of whole wheat bread. Cut each sandwich in half to form finger sandwiches. Yield: 2 dozen.

OLIVE-CHEESE SANDWICHES

1 egg, lightly beaten
¼ cup vinegar
2 tablespoons sugar
1 tablespoon butter or
   margarine
¼ teaspoon salt
¼ teaspoon pepper
4 cups (16 ounces) shredded
   Cheddar cheese
1 (3-ounce) jar
   pimiento-stuffed olives,
   drained and chopped
27 slices pumpernickel bread,
   crust removed
Sliced pimiento-stuffed olives
   (optional)

Combine egg, vinegar, sugar, butter, salt, and pepper in top of a double boiler; cook over boiling water, stirring constantly, 3 minutes or until thickened. Remove from heat, and cool to room temperature. Stir in cheese and chopped olives. Cover and chill.

Cut each bread slice into 4 triangles. Spread 1 heaping teaspoon cheese mixture on each triangle. Garnish each with an olive slice, if desired. Yield: 9 dozen.

ALMOND MERINGUE COOKIES

1 cup all-purpose flour
¼ teaspoon salt
¼ cup plus 2 tablespoons
  shortening
2 to 3 tablespoons cold water
2 egg whites
¼ teaspoon almond extract
2 tablespoons plus 1½
  teaspoons sugar
Cherry preserves
Toasted chopped almonds

Combine flour and salt in a small mixing bowl; cut in shortening with a pastry blender until mixture resembles coarse meal. Sprinkle water evenly over surface of flour mixture; stir with a fork until dry ingredients are moistened. Shape dough into a ball; chill.

Turn dough out onto a lightly floured surface, and roll to ⅛-inch thickness. Cut with a 2-inch diamond-shaped cookie cutter; place on ungreased cookie sheets. Bake at 475° for 6 to 8 minutes or until lightly browned. Remove from cookie sheets, and cool on wire racks.

Combine egg whites (at room temperature) and almond extract; beat until foamy. Gradually add sugar, beating until stiff peaks form and sugar dissolves. Set aside.

Spoon ½ teaspoon preserves into center of each cookie. Spread a small amount of meringue over preserves, covering entire surface of each cookie. Sprinkle with chopped almonds. Return cookies to cookie sheets, and bake at 425° for 6 minutes or until meringue is lightly browned. Remove from cookie sheets, and cool on wire racks. Yield: 2 dozen.

To go with a pot of tea, a double treat: Almond Meringue Cookies in which pastry and meringue conceal a cherry filling.

CHOCOLATE-MOCHA CHEESECAKES

30 vanilla wafers
8 (1-ounce) squares
  semisweet chocolate
1 (8-ounce) carton
  commercial sour cream,
  divided
4 (8-ounce) packages cream
  cheese, softened
1 cup sugar
2 eggs
½ cup strong coffee
1 teaspoon vanilla
  extract
Grated semisweet chocolate

Place one vanilla wafer in the bottom of each paper-lined muffin pan; set aside.

Place chocolate squares in top of a double boiler. Cook over boiling water, stirring frequently, until chocolate melts. Remove from heat; add 2 tablespoons sour cream, stirring well. Set aside.

Beat cream cheese in a large mixing bowl with an electric mixer until light and fluffy. Gradually add sugar; mix well. Add eggs; beat well. Add reserved chocolate mixture, coffee, and vanilla, beating at low speed of electric mixer until well blended. Fold in remaining sour cream.

Spoon batter evenly into prepared muffin pans, filling three-fourths full. Bake at 350° for 25 minutes; cool completely on wire racks. Chill overnight.

Remove paper lining from each cheesecake, and garnish with grated chocolate. Serve chilled. Yield: 2½ dozen.

STUFFED DRIED FRUIT

½ (8-ounce) package pitted
  dates
3 pecan halves
3 walnut halves
3 whole almonds
3 peanuts
1 (3-ounce) package cream
  cheese, softened
½ (6-ounce) package dried
  apricots
¼ cup sugar

Make a lengthwise slit in dates. Stuff each with one type of nut; set aside.

Beat cream cheese in a small mixing bowl until light and fluffy. Spread 1 teaspoon cream cheese on half of apricots; top with remaining apricots.

Roll reserved dates and stuffed apricots in sugar. Yield: 12 servings.

A 1910 souvenir from the Crystal Palace, Galveston.

ALMOND MERINGUE COOKIES

1 cup all-purpose flour
¼ teaspoon salt
¼ cup plus 2 tablespoons shortening
2 to 3 tablespoons cold water
2 egg whites
¼ teaspoon almond extract
2 tablespoons plus 1½ teaspoons sugar
Cherry preserves
Toasted chopped almonds

Combine flour and salt in a small mixing bowl; cut in shortening with a pastry blender until mixture resembles coarse meal. Sprinkle water evenly over surface of flour mixture; stir with a fork until dry ingredients are moistened. Shape dough into a ball; chill.

Turn dough out onto a lightly floured surface, and roll to ⅛-inch thickness. Cut with a 2-inch diamond-shaped cookie cutter; place on ungreased cookie sheets. Bake at 475° for 6 to 8 minutes or until lightly browned. Remove from cookie sheets, and cool on wire racks.

Combine egg whites (at room temperature) and almond extract; beat until foamy. Gradually add sugar, beating until stiff peaks form and sugar dissolves. Set aside.

Spoon ½ teaspoon preserves into center of each cookie. Spread a small amount of meringue over preserves, covering entire surface of each cookie. Sprinkle with chopped almonds. Return cookies to cookie sheets, and bake at 425° for 6 minutes or until meringue is lightly browned. Remove from cookie sheets, and cool on wire racks. Yield: 2 dozen.

To go with a pot of tea, a double treat: Almond Meringue Cookies in which pastry and meringue conceal a cherry filling.

CHOCOLATE-MOCHA CHEESECAKES

30 vanilla wafers
8 (1-ounce) squares semisweet chocolate
1 (8-ounce) carton commercial sour cream, divided
4 (8-ounce) packages cream cheese, softened
1 cup sugar
2 eggs
½ cup strong coffee
1 teaspoon vanilla extract
Grated semisweet chocolate

Place one vanilla wafer in the bottom of each paper-lined muffin pan; set aside.

Place chocolate squares in top of a double boiler. Cook over boiling water, stirring frequently, until chocolate melts. Remove from heat; add 2 tablespoons sour cream, stirring well. Set aside.

Beat cream cheese in a large mixing bowl with an electric mixer until light and fluffy. Gradually add sugar; mix well. Add eggs; beat well. Add reserved chocolate mixture, coffee, and vanilla, beating at low speed of electric mixer until well blended. Fold in remaining sour cream.

Spoon batter evenly into prepared muffin pans, filling three-fourths full. Bake at 350° for 25 minutes; cool completely on wire racks. Chill overnight.

Remove paper lining from each cheesecake, and garnish with grated chocolate. Serve chilled. Yield: 2½ dozen.

STUFFED DRIED FRUIT

½ (8-ounce) package pitted dates
3 pecan halves
3 walnut halves
3 whole almonds
3 peanuts
1 (3-ounce) package cream cheese, softened
½ (6-ounce) package dried apricots
¼ cup sugar

Make a lengthwise slit in dates. Stuff each with one type of nut; set aside.

Beat cream cheese in a small mixing bowl until light and fluffy. Spread 1 teaspoon cream cheese on half of apricots; top with remaining apricots.

Roll reserved dates and stuffed apricots in sugar. Yield: 12 servings.

A 1910 souvenir from the Crystal Palace, Galveston.

Houston Metropolitan Research Center, Houston Public Library

BREAKFAST PARTY FOR MRS. McKINLEY

On June 12, 1897, the women of Nashville's Centennial Club hosted a breakfast in honor of Mrs. William McKinley, which was, in the words of a *Nashville American* reporter, " . . . distinctively the social feature of the Centennial Period." It was noted that the First Lady looked pale from fatigue; it must have been with relief that she found her chair, which was wreathed in asparagus vines. A profusion of white roses and sweet peas filled the hall. Myriads of tiny electric lights shone from the ceiling — and such a breakfast: fish timbales, ices, cakes. . . . The fish course in party menus frequently took the form of timbales. Here we have substituted Cornish hens, a twentieth-century development, for the chicken on the McKinley menu.

FRESH ORANGE SECTIONS WITH MINT GARNISH
FISH PUDDING
or
CORNISH HENS WITH BACON
MUSHROOM GRAVY
GREEN PEAS IN TOMATO CUPS
LUNCHEON ICEBOX ROLLS
CHOCOLATE SPRITZ COOKIES
STRAWBERRY ICE
COFFEE

Serves 8

FISH PUDDING

2 pounds red snapper fillets or other mild, white fish
2 quarts water
1 large onion, sliced
1 bay leaf
1 tablespoon vinegar
1 teapoon salt
4 slices white bread
1 cup cold water
1 medium onion, chopped
3 tablespoons butter or margarine, separated
2 tablespoons all-purpose flour
2 cups milk
2 eggs
2 tablespoons Worcestershire sauce
2 teaspoons salt
½ teaspoon white pepper
Fresh parsley sprigs (optional)
Lemon wedges (optional)
Mushroom Gravy (page 25)

Rinse fish thoroughly in cold water; pat dry, and set aside.

Combine 2 quarts water, sliced onion, bay leaf, vinegar, and 1 teaspoon salt in a large Dutch oven; bring to a boil. Boil, uncovered, 10 minutes. Add fish, and simmer, uncovered, 8 minutes or until fish flakes easily when tested with a fork.

Carefully remove fish from liquid; drain. Discard cooking liquid and vegetables. Remove and discard skin from fish, and place fish in a large mixing bowl; flake fish, using a fork. Set aside.

Soak bread slices in 1 cup water in a small, shallow baking pan until all liquid is absorbed; press excess water from each bread slice, and crumble over reserved fish, mixing well.

Sauté chopped onion in 1 tablespoon butter in a small skillet until tender; drain. Add to fish mixture, stirring well.

Melt remaining butter in a heavy saucepan over low heat; add flour, stirring until smooth. Gradually add milk; cook over medium heat, stirring constantly, until thickened and bubbly.

Beat eggs in a small mixing bowl until light and lemon colored; gradually add one-fourth of hot milk mixture to eggs, beating with a wire whisk. Add to remaining hot mixture, stirring constantly. Cook, stirring constantly, until mixture thickens. Remove from heat.

Add hot mixture, Worcestershire sauce, 2 teaspoons salt, and pepper to reserved fish mixture; stir well.

Spoon mixture into a lightly oiled 5½-cup ring mold; press mixture evenly into mold. Place mold in a 13- x 9- x 2-inch baking pan; pour hot water into pan to a depth of 1 inch. Bake at 350° for 35 minutes or until set. Remove from oven; turn pudding out onto a serving platter, and garnish with parsley and lemon wedges, if desired. Serve immediately with Mushroom Gravy. Yield: 8 servings.

CORNISH HENS WITH BACON

4 (1½-pound) Cornish hens
¼ cup butter or margarine
Salt to taste
Pepper to taste
4 slices bacon, cut in half and
   partially cooked
Mushroom Gravy

Remove giblets from hens; reserve for other uses. Rinse hens with cold water, and pat dry. Split each hen lengthwise, using a sharp knife. Rub hens with butter; sprinkle with salt and pepper. Place hens, cavity side up, on a rack in a shallow roasting pan. Bake at 350° for 1 hour, turning once.

Remove hens from oven; place one half slice of bacon across each hen. Return to oven, and broil 5 minutes or until bacon is crisp. Serve hens with Mushroom Gravy. Yield: 8 servings.

MUSHROOM GRAVY

½ small onion, chopped
2 tablespoons butter or
   margarine
2½ tablespoons all-purpose
   flour
1 cup beef broth
1 (4-ounce) can sliced
   mushrooms, drained
Dash of salt
Dash of pepper

Sauté onion in butter in a small skillet until lightly browned. Remove and discard onion. Add flour to butter; cook over low heat 1 minute, stirring constantly. Gradually add broth; cook over medium heat, stirring constantly, until thickened and bubbly. Stir in mushrooms, salt, and pepper. Yield: 1½ cups.

GREEN PEAS IN TOMATO CUPS

8 firm ripe tomatoes
⅔ cup chopped onion
1 tablespoon butter or
   margarine
1 teaspoon dried whole
   basil
½ teaspoon salt
1 pound cooked green peas

Remove stems from tomatoes, and cut a ½-inch slice from the top of each. Scoop out pulp, leaving shells intact; reserve pulp for other uses. Invert tomato shells onto paper towels to drain. Transfer tomatoes to a shallow baking pan, and broil 8 inches from heating element for 5 minutes; set aside.

Sauté onion in butter in a small skillet until tender. Combine sautéed onion, basil, salt, and green peas; toss lightly. Spoon pea mixture evenly into reserved tomato shells. Serve immediately. Yield: 8 servings.

A very colorful idea: Cornish Hens for an all-out party breakfast, with Green Peas in Tomato Cups and Luncheon Icebox Rolls.

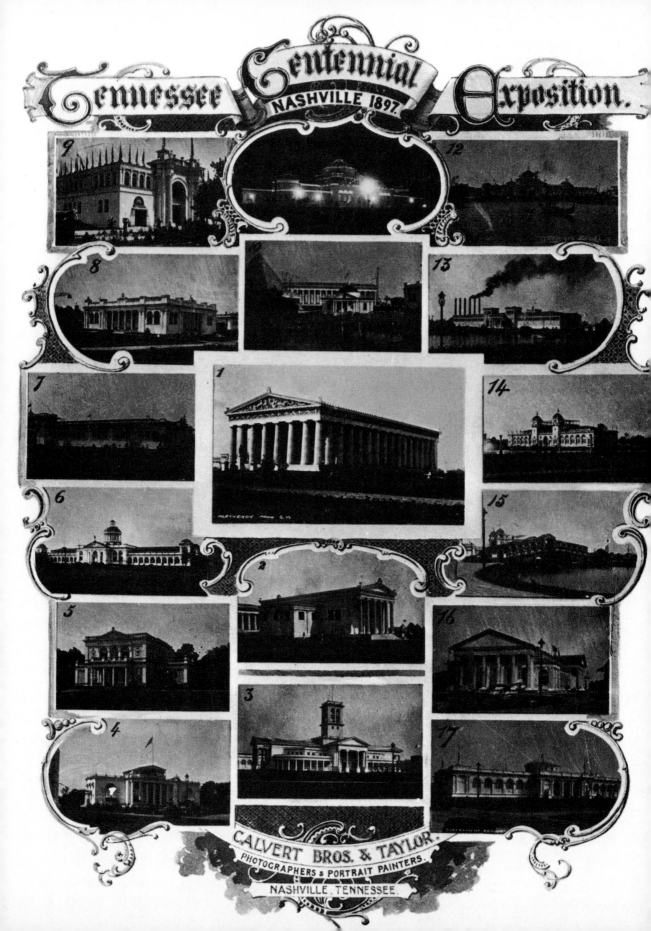

Tennessee Centennial Exposition.

NASHVILLE 1897.

CALVERT BROS. & TAYLOR.
PHOTOGRAPHERS & PORTRAIT PAINTERS.
NASHVILLE, TENNESSEE.

LUNCHEON ICEBOX ROLLS

2 cups milk
½ cup sugar
½ cup shortening
1 package dry yeast
1 teaspoon baking powder
½ teaspoon baking soda
1 tablespoon salt
5 cups all-purpose flour, divided
Melted butter or margarine

Combine milk, sugar, and shortening in a medium saucepan; bring to a boil. Remove from heat, and cool to lukewarm (105° to 115°).

Combine yeast, baking powder, soda, salt, and 2 cups flour in a large mixing bowl, mixing well; add milk mixture, stirring well. Cover and let rise in a warm place (85°), free from drafts, 1½ hours or until doubled in bulk.

Add remaining flour, stirring well. Cover and refrigerate overnight.

Turn dough out onto a lightly floured surface; knead 10 to 12 times. Roll to ¼-inch thickness. Cut with a 2-inch biscuit cutter; brush with melted butter. Make a crease across each circle, and fold one half over. Gently press edges together to seal. Place rolls on lightly greased baking sheets; cover and repeat rising procedure 20 minutes or until doubled in bulk. Bake at 400° for 8 to 10 minutes or until golden brown. Yield: about 3 dozen.

Ida Saxton McKinley was a woman of indomitable will, plagued by ill health. For White House entertaining, she conserved her strength for enormous dinners and receptions. Her husband, against protocol, sat beside her at table in case she became ill, taking care of her when she did. McKinley was assassinated in 1901.

CHOCOLATE SPRITZ COOKIES

1 cup butter or margarine, softened
¾ cup sugar
1 egg
1 teaspoon vanilla extract
2¼ cups all-purpose flour
¼ cup plus 2 tablespoons cocoa
½ teaspoon baking powder
⅛ teaspoon salt

Cream butter; gradually add sugar, beating until light and fluffy. Add egg; beat well. Stir in vanilla.

Sift together flour, cocoa, baking powder, and salt; stir into creamed mixture.

Use a cookie press to shape dough into desired shapes. Place cookies on ungreased cookie sheets. Bake at 400° for 8 to 10 minutes. Remove cookies to wire racks to cool. Yield: about 5 dozen.

STRAWBERRY ICE

1 quart water
3 cups fresh strawberries, cleaned and hulled
1½ cups sugar
Juice of ½ lemon
3 drops red food coloring

Combine all ingredients in a large saucepan; stir well. Bring to a boil; cook over high heat 5 minutes, stirring frequently. Remove from heat, and cool.

Pour strawberry mixture into container of an electric blender; process until smooth. Pour mixture into the freezer can of a 1-gallon hand-turned or electric freezer. Freeze according to manufacturer's instructions. Let ripen 1 hour before serving. Yield: 3 quarts.

Mrs. McKinley accepted a breakfast invitation sent her by the ladies of Nashville's Centennial Club.

New York Public Library

FOR LADIES ONLY

Vegetable Soup and Apple Butter Muffins from a convenient make-ahead menu. Meat for the soup is better cooked, the broth chilled, and the fat removed before the vegetables are added.

Parties "for ladies only" took root in that most practical of soils, necessity. Just as men came together in the early days of the South to raise barns or to help with hog-killing, the women met to quilt, prepare fruit for drying or, in war times, to sew for their soldiers. Women were not self-conscious about their roles then; with rare exceptions, they did "women's work" as it had been cut out for them by their mothers.

Church women's auxiliaries turned their hands to group efforts early on, using their home-based talents to raise funds for missionary efforts, building and grounds improvements, and orphans' homes. They gave dinners and luncheons, held bake sales, and sewed for those orphanages. Through such group associations, women became increasingly aware of the possibility for personal growth. With urbanization, garden clubs grew out of neighborly seed-swapping; as pride in their surroundings spread from street to town, those women went from "Let's take time out for coffee" to serious meetings in homes and, eventually, in clubhouses. But always, always, with splendid food. Looking outside their homes, women discovered culture and style. They read Richard Harding Davis, emulated Charles Dana Gibson's "girl," and enjoyed performances by stage greats John Drew, Maude Adams, and E. H. Sutherland.

From study, sewing, gardening, and other modest but special interest groups, women have evolved power structures, which can save and maintain a historic shrine; charity fund-raising teams, which can transform an abandoned armory into a Pacific Island for a $200-per-person ball; and politically informed lobbies, which can influence governments from the local to the national level.

Women, despite their varied roles today, gather to ponder common goals or simply to have fun. Notably, the evolved Southern woman can slip with ease from her work mode into her charitable club endeavors. And when she's in the mood, she can still give a coffee or chafing dish luncheon or teatime collation with a finesse that would make her late great-grandmother proud.

QUILTING BEE LUNCHEON

Generations ago, when the South was almost totally rural, women met for quilting bees to help one another put the finishing touch on their hand-pieced "tops." Lined up three or four to a side of the quilting frame, they made invisibly small stitches into a carefully drawn pattern. Whig Rose, Double Wedding Ring, Jacob's Ladder, Drunkard's Path, Lone Star of Texas, Flower Garden, Log Cabin . . . the surviving examples, stuffed with cotton and sometimes backed by cloth made on the farm, are beyond price. Revival of interest in the quilting art is in progress. The nimble-fingered quilters, again, are meeting to work and to socialize over lunch.

VEGETABLE SOUP
APPLE BUTTER MUFFINS
MARBLE LOAF CAKE
VANILLA PUDDING

Serves 8

The Quilting Party, an oil depicting an heirloom in production, c.1854.

VEGETABLE SOUP

3 quarts water
1 meaty beef
  shank bone
1 tablespoon salt
1 (28-ounce) can whole
  tomatoes, undrained and
  chopped
3 cups sliced okra
2 cups fresh lima beans
1½ cups whole kernel
  corn
1 cup chopped onion
1 cup diced celery

Combine water, shank bone, and salt in a large stock pot; bring to a boil. Skim surface, and reduce heat. Cover and simmer 1 hour or until meat is tender.

Remove soup bone from broth. Remove meat, and cut into bite-size pieces, discarding bone. Return meat to broth; bring to a boil. Stir in remaining ingredients. Reduce heat; cover and simmer 1½ hours. Serve hot. Yield: 1 gallon.

APPLE BUTTER MUFFINS

1 egg, well beaten
1 cup milk
1 cup all-purpose flour
1 cup whole wheat flour
1 tablespoon plus 1 teaspoon
  baking powder
1 teaspoon salt
2 tablespoons firmly
  packed brown sugar
1 cup raisins
2 tablespoons shortening,
  melted
½ cup apple butter

Combine egg and milk in a large mixing bowl; stir well.

Combine flour, baking powder, salt, sugar, and raisins in a medium mixing bowl; add to egg mixture, stirring just until dry ingredients are moistened.

Add shortening and apple butter, stirring just until blended. Spoon batter into a greased muffin pan, filling two-thirds full. Bake at 400° for 20 minutes or until golden brown. Yield: 1 dozen.

MARBLE LOAF CAKE

½ cup butter or margarine,
  softened
1 cup sugar
3 eggs, separated
2 teaspoons vanilla extract,
  divided
2¼ cups all-purpose flour
2 teaspoons baking powder
1 cup milk
3 (1-ounce) squares
  semisweet chocolate,
  melted
½ cup sifted powdered sugar
1 tablespoon half-and-half

Cream butter in a large mixing bowl; gradually add 1 cup sugar, beating well. Add egg yolks and 1½ teaspoons vanilla; beat well.

Combine flour and baking powder; stir well. Add to creamed mixture alternately with milk, beginning and ending with flour mixture.

Beat egg whites (at room temperature) until stiff peaks form; fold into batter. Divide batter in half; add melted chocolate to one half. Spoon one-fourth of chocolate batter into a greased 9- x 5- x 3-inch loafpan; top with one-fourth of plain batter. Repeat layers until all batter is used. Gently cut through batter in zigzag fashion in several places, using a spatula. Bake at 350° for 1 hour and 10 minutes or until a wooden pick inserted in center comes out clean. Cool in pan 15 minutes; remove loaf from pan, and cool completely on a wire rack.

Combine powdered sugar, half-and-half, and ½ teaspoon vanilla in a small mixing bowl; beat until smooth. Spoon glaze evenly over cake. Slice and serve. Yield: one 9-inch loaf.

Make-aheads: Vanilla Pudding and Marble Loaf Cake.

VANILLA PUDDING

¼ cup cornstarch
4½ cups milk, divided
¾ cup sugar
Dash of salt
2 eggs, lightly beaten
1 teaspoon vanilla extract
Strawberries (optional)

Dissolve cornstarch in ½ cup milk; set aside.

Bring remaining milk to a boil in top of a double boiler over boiling water, stirring constantly. Reduce heat, and stir in cornstarch mixture, sugar, and salt. Gradually stir one-fourth of hot mixture into eggs; add to remaining hot mixture, stirring constantly. Bring to a boil over low heat, stirring constantly. Cook 1 minute; remove from heat, and stir in vanilla. Cool to room temperature; chill.

Spoon pudding into individual serving bowls. Garnish with strawberries, if desired. Yield: 8 servings.

WOMAN'S STUDY CLUB MEETING

There had been ladies' clubs before the "Gay Nineties," but the married woman's card clubs and euchre clubs had been for recreation only. Near the turn of the century, study groups were growing in Southern cities. "Beauty Or Brains The Stronger Power in Women?" as the topic of one such group in Savannah in the 1890s shows stirrings of feminism. In Garland, Texas, a woman's study club founded in 1897 is still going strong. Members traditionally answer roll call by following a pre-selected theme: "I remember when . . . ," or "did you know that . . . ?" Refreshments usually consist of a hearty meat salad and a rich dessert.

CONGEALED TOMATO-TUNA SALAD
SNOWBALLS
ICED MINT TEA

Serves 10 to 12

CONGEALED TOMATO-TUNA SALAD

1 (10¾-ounce) can tomato soup, undiluted
2 (3-ounce) packages cream cheese
2 envelopes unflavored gelatin
½ cup cold water
½ cup chopped pecans
½ cup chopped celery
½ cup chopped green pepper
½ cup chopped onion
½ cup sliced pimiento-stuffed olives
1 (6½-ounce) can tuna, drained and flaked
1 cup mayonnaise
Lettuce leaves

Bring soup to a boil in a medium saucepan. Add cream cheese; cook over medium heat, stirring constantly, until cream cheese melts.

Soften gelatin in cold water; let stand 5 minutes. Add to soup mixture, stirring until gelatin dissolves. Remove from heat, and let cool to room temperature. Stir in pecans, celery, green pepper, onion, olives, and tuna. Fold in mayonnaise.

Pour mixture into lightly oiled individual molds. Chill until firm. Unmold salad onto individual lettuce-lined plates. Yield: 10 to 12 servings.

Congealed Tomato-Tuna Salad with cooling Mint Tea.

A Houston study and literary society dressed in allegorical costumes, c.1920.

SNOWBALLS

½ cup sugar
½ cup chopped pecans
1 egg, lightly beaten
½ (8-ounce) can crushed
  pineapple, drained
2 tablespoons butter or
  margarine
Dash of salt
1 (12-ounce) package vanilla
  wafers
1 cup whipping cream
1 tablespoon plus 1½
  teaspoons sugar
1 (7-ounce) package flaked
  coconut

Combine ½ cup sugar, pecans, egg, pineapple, butter, and salt in a medium saucepan; mix well. Cook over medium heat, stirring constantly, until mixture thickens. Cool to room temperature.

Using 3 vanilla wafers per serving, spread pineapple mixture between wafers sandwich-style. Cover tightly, and refrigerate overnight.

Beat whipping cream until foamy; gradually add 1 tablespoon plus 1½ teaspoons sugar, beating until soft peaks form.

Frost top and sides of each stack of wafers with whipped cream; sprinkle liberally with coconut. Chill until serving time. To serve, place on individual serving dishes. Yield: 10 to 12 servings.

ICED MINT TEA

7 regular-size tea bags
12 sprigs fresh mint
Grated rind of 3 lemons
2 quarts boiling water
Juice of 7 lemons
  (about 1 cup)
2 cups sugar
2 quarts water
Fresh mint leaves
Lemon slices

Combine tea bags, mint sprigs, lemon rind, and 2 quarts boiling water in a large glass container; cover and steep 12 minutes. Remove and discard tea bags. Add lemon juice and sugar, stirring until sugar dissolves. Strain tea; add water.

Serve tea over ice, and garnish each serving with mint leaves and lemon slices. Yield: 1 gallon.

VERANDA LUNCHEON

Happy is the woman who possesses a veranda" is the opening line of a chapter in *Easy Entertaining*, 1911. Verandas are seldom featured in house plans anymore, but we all know such delightfully serene spots. We envision verandas we have enjoyed and see chintz pillows against wrought iron or wicker furniture painted bright white, lots of fresh flowers, of course (daffodils are gorgeous in April), and pitchers of frosty beverages to drink with an unusually feminine menu. Even without a veranda, we can still live up to the outdoor spirit with one of its modern replacements: a deck or a patio to allow our guests the pleasure of an airy setting.

FROZEN FRUIT SALAD
or
FRESH FRUIT SALAD
WITH HORSERADISH DRESSING
CHEESE STRATA
PECAN TARTS
ICED TEA PUNCH

Serves 10

FROZEN FRUIT SALAD

1 (17½-ounce) can Royal Anne cherries, drained and chopped
1 (17-ounce) can apricot halves, drained and chopped
1 (8½-ounce) can pear halves, drained and chopped
1 (8-ounce) can pineapple tidbits, drained
1 (6-ounce) can maraschino cherries, drained and chopped
4 medium oranges, peeled, sectioned, seeded, and cut into bite-size pieces
2 bananas, peeled and sliced
¾ cup chopped pecans
2 eggs
¼ cup cider vinegar
¼ cup sugar
20 large marshmallows
1 cup whipping cream
Lettuce leaves

Combine first 8 ingredients in a large mixing bowl; cover and refrigerate.

Combine eggs, vinegar, and sugar in top of a double boiler; beat well. Cook over boiling water, stirring constantly, until thickened and bubby. Remove from heat; add marshmallows, stirring until marshmallows melt. Let cool completely.

Beat whipping cream until stiff peaks form; fold into cooled marshmallow mixture.

Drain fruit thoroughly. Fold in whipped cream mixture. Pour into a lightly oiled 9-cup mold. Cover and freeze 24 hours. Let stand at room temperature 15 minutes; turn salad out onto a lettuce-lined plate. Slice and serve immediately. Yield: 10 servings.

FRESH FRUIT SALAD WITH HORSERADISH DRESSING

4 oranges, peeled, sectioned, and seeded
4 peaches, peeled, seeded, and sliced
2 grapefruits, sectioned
1 pineapple, peeled, cored, and cut into chunks
2 cups red seedless grapes
Lettuce leaves
Horseradish Dressing

Combine orange sections, peach slices, grapefruit sections, pineapple chunks, and grapes in a large mixing bowl; toss lightly. Arrange fruit on lettuce-lined serving dishes. Serve with Horseradish Dressing. Yield: 10 servings.

Horseradish Dressing:

¼ cup whipping cream, whipped
½ cup mayonnaise
1 to 2 tablespoons prepared horseradish

Combine whipping cream, mayonnaise, and horseradish in a small mixing bowl; stir well, and chill. Yield: about 1 cup.

Frozen Fruit Salad, Cheese Strata, Pecan Tarts, and Iced Tea Pun

Ladies relax over refreshments on a Louisville veranda, 1928.

CHEESE STRATA

10 slices bread, crust
   removed
2 tablespoons butter or
   margarine, melted
2½ cups milk
4 eggs, lightly beaten
2 cups (8 ounces) shredded
   sharp Cheddar cheese
½ teaspoon salt
Tomato rose (optional)
Fresh parsley sprigs (optional)

Cut bread into cubes, and
toss with melted butter. Place
bread evenly in a buttered 12- x
8- x 2-inch baking pan. Combine milk, eggs, cheese, and salt
in a large mixing bowl, stirring
until well blended; pour evenly
over bread cubes. Cover and refrigerate overnight.

Uncover and bake at 350° for
40 minutes. Cut into 10 equal
portions, and garnish with a tomato rose and parsley, if desired. Serve immediately. Yield:
10 servings.

PECAN TARTS

¼ cup butter or margarine,
   melted
½ cup light corn syrup
½ cup sugar
2 eggs, beaten
1 teaspoon vanilla extract
Dash of salt
1¼ cups finely chopped
   pecans
10 unbaked (2¾-inch) tart
   shells

Combine first 6 ingredients;
beat well. Stir in pecans. Pour
filling evenly into tart shells.
Bake at 350° for 30 minutes or
until set. Yield: 10 tarts.

ICED TEA PUNCH

2 (12-ounce) cans frozen
   lemonade concentrate,
   undiluted
3½ quarts water
½ cup tea leaves
½ cup sugar
Lemon slices

Combine lemonade concen-
trate and water in a large saucepan; bring to a boil. Remove
from heat; add tea leaves. Cover
and steep 5 minutes. Strain and
discard tea leaves. Stir in sugar;
cool. Pour punch over ice in
glasses, and garnish with lemon
slices. Yield: 1 gallon.

CHAFING DISH LUNCHEON

By 1907, when the *Rumford Cookbook* devoted an entire chapter to chafing dish cookery, hostesses discovered they could prepare part of a company dinner without absenting themselves from the table. For precooked foods, such as Creamed Sweetbreads or Welsh Rarebit, that need only to be kept hot or for foods that need only the gentlest of heat to finish, the water basin is used between the flame and the food pan. This menu comes from *How We Cook In Tennessee*, 1900.

CAVIAR CANAPÉS * CLAMS IN BOUILLON
OLIVES * RADISHES
WELSH RAREBIT ON TOAST POINTS
or
CREAMED SWEETBREADS OVER LUNCHEON BISCUITS
WALDORF SALAD
WINE JELLY WITH SABAYON SAUCE

Serves 12

CAVIAR CANAPÉS

3 eggs
¼ cup milk
½ teaspoon salt
¼ teaspoon pepper
2 tablespoons butter or
   margarine
6 slices bread
Additional butter or margarine
1 (3½-ounce) jar red lumpfish
   caviar
1 tablespoon whipping cream

Combine eggs, milk, salt, and pepper in a shallow bowl, beating well.

Melt 2 tablespoons butter in a large skillet. Dip 2 bread slices into egg mixture, coating well; drain, and place in skillet. Cook over medium heat 4 minutes on each side or until browned. Remove from skillet. Cut each slice into 4 circles with a 1½-inch biscuit cutter. Keep warm. Repeat procedure with remaining bread slices, adding additional butter to skillet as needed.

Combine caviar and whipping cream in a small saucepan; cook over medium heat 2 minutes, stirring constantly. Spoon ½ teaspoon caviar mixture over each French toast circle. Serve immediately. Yield: 12 servings.

Cover of a booklet of chafing dish recipes, 1897.

THE CHAFING DISH

CLAMS IN BOUILLON

6 pounds lean, cubed beef
1½ gallons water
1 (14½-ounce) can tomatoes,
  undrained
1 tablespoon salt
1 tablespoon celery seed
½ teaspoon whole allspice
½ teaspoon whole cloves
1 sweet red pepper, seeded
1 bay leaf
1 clove garlic
1 onion, coarsely chopped
1 carrot, scraped and chopped
¼ teaspoon dried whole
  thyme
2 eggs
3 (6½-ounce) cans minced
  clams, drained and rinsed

Combine first 10 ingredients in a large stockpot. Bring to a boil; skim surface. Reduce heat; cover and simmer 2½ hours.

Add onion, carrot, and thyme. Cover and simmer 2½ hours. Remove from heat, and cool. Strain through several layers of damp cheesecloth, discarding vegetables and spices. (Reserve beef for other uses.) Cover and refrigerate overnight.

Skim off and discard any fat which has risen to surface. Separate eggs, reserving yolks for other uses. Coarsely crumble egg shells; combine shells and whites in a medium mixing bowl. Gradually pour 1 cup bouillon into whites, stirring well. Return egg mixture to remaining bouillon; bring to a boil. Cook over high heat 10 minutes. Remove from heat; let stand 5 minutes.

Strain mixture through several layers of damp cheesecloth, discarding egg shells. Return bouillon to stockpot, and stir in clams; cook until thoroughly heated. Ladle into individual serving bowls; serve immediately. Yield: about 3 quarts.

Note: Clams in Bouillon may be served as an appetizer soup or with the meal.

Chafing dish cookery in the dorm, Brenau College, Gainesville, Georgia, 1912.

WELSH RAREBIT ON TOAST POINTS

4 cups (16 ounces) shredded
  process American cheese
⅓ cup beer
2 eggs, well beaten
2 teaspoons Worcestershire
  sauce
1 teaspoon salt
½ teaspoon paprika
Dash of pepper
Toast points
Additional beer

Place cheese in top of a double boiler. Cook over simmering water, stirring constantly, until cheese melts. Gradually add beer, beating with a wire whisk, until mixture is smooth.

Combine eggs, Worcestershire sauce, salt, paprika, and pepper. Add to hot mixture; stir until smooth and thickened.

Transfer to a chafing dish; keep warm. Stir, and add additional beer, as needed. Serve on toast points. Yield: 12 servings.

Welsh Rarebit and Waldorf Salad: quick and good.

CREAMED SWEETBREADS OVER LUNCHEON BISCUITS

2 pounds veal sweetbreads
2 tablespoons lemon juice
1 teaspoon salt
2 (4-ounce) cans sliced
  mushrooms, undrained
¼ cup chopped shallots
2 tablespoons chopped fresh
  parsley
½ cup butter or margarine
¼ cup plus 2 tablespoons
  all-purpose flour
2 cups milk, scalded
4 egg yolks
¼ cup sherry
2 tablespoons Worcestershire
  sauce
Dash of hot sauce
Luncheon Biscuits

Soak sweetbreads in water to cover 1 hour. Drain; remove and discard membranes. Combine sweetbreads, water to cover, lemon juice, and salt in a medium Dutch oven. Bring to a boil. Reduce heat; cover and simmer 30 minutes. Rinse sweetbreads with cold water. Cool; cut into ½-inch pieces.

Drain mushrooms, reserving ½ cup liquid; set aside.

Sauté shallots and parsley in butter in a medium saucepan until tender; add flour, stirring until well blended. Cook over medium heat 1 minute, stirring constantly. Gradually add milk and reserved mushroom liquid; cook over medium heat, stirring constantly, until thickened and bubbly. Stir in mushrooms and sweetbreads; simmer 10 minutes, stirring frequently.

Beat egg yolks until thick and lemon colored. Gradually stir one-fourth of hot mixture into yolks; add to remaining hot mixture, stirring constantly. Cook over medium heat, stirring constantly, until mixture thickens.

Remove from heat, and stir in sherry, Worcestershire sauce, and hot sauce. Transfer hot sweetbreads mixture to a chafing dish; keep warm. Serve immediately over Luncheon Biscuits. Yield: 12 servings.

Luncheon Biscuits:

2¾ cups all-purpose
  flour
1 tablespoon baking
  powder
1 teaspoon salt
½ cup plus 1 tablespoon
  shortening
1 cup milk
Melted butter or margarine

Sift together flour, baking powder, and salt in a medium mixing bowl. Cut in shortening with a pastry blender until mixture resembles coarse meal. Gradually add milk, stirring just until dry ingredients are moistened. Shape into a ball.

Turn dough out onto a lightly floured surface; knead 10 to 12 times. Roll to ½-inch thickness; cut with a 1¾-inch biscuit cutter. Place biscuits on lightly greased baking sheets; brush with melted butter. Bake at 450° for 10 minutes or until lightly browned. Serve warm. Yield: 2½ dozen.

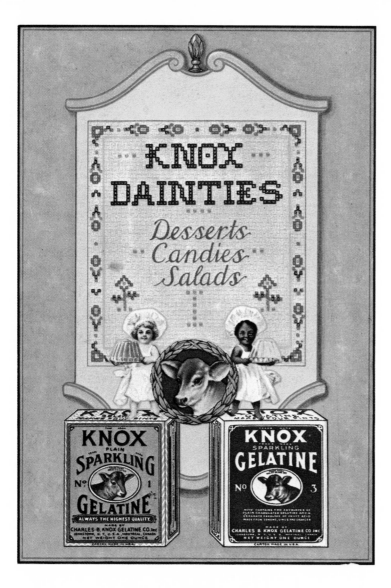

WINE JELLY WITH SABAYON SAUCE

2 envelopes unflavored
  gelatin
1½ cups water, divided
⅔ cup sugar
2 cups sherry
¼ cup orange juice
¼ cup lemon juice
Dash of salt
Sabayon Sauce

Soften gelatin in ½ cup cold water. Bring remaining water to a boil in a heavy saucepan. Remove from heat. Stir in softened gelatin and next 5 ingredients, stirring until gelatin and sugar dissolve.

Pour mixture into a lightly oiled 4-cup mold, and refrigerate overnight. Unmold jelly on a serving plate. Slice and serve with Sabayon Sauce. Yield: 12 servings.

Sabayon Sauce:

8 egg yolks
1 cup sugar
⅛ teaspoon salt
1 cup sherry
1 tablespoon lemon juice
2 teaspoons brandy
1 cup whipping cream,
  whipped

Beat egg yolks and sugar in top of a double boiler; add salt. Gradually add sherry, lemon juice, and brandy. Cook over simmering water, stirring constantly with a wire whisk, until thick and creamy. Remove from heat; cool to room temperature. Refrigerate until thoroughly chilled.

Fold whipped cream into chilled mixture. Cover and refrigerate until needed. Yield: about 1 quart.

WALDORF SALAD

¾ cup sugar
¾ teaspoon all-purpose
  flour
¼ cup plus 2 tablespoons
  milk
¼ cup plus 2 tablespoons
  vinegar
1 egg, lightly beaten
3 tablespoons butter or
  margarine
¾ teaspoon salt
¾ teaspoon prepared mustard
6 apples, cored and chopped
4 stalks celery, chopped
2 cups coarsely chopped
  walnuts
Celery leaves (optional)
Walnut halves (optional)

Combine sugar and flour in a non-metal saucepan; mix well. Add milk, vinegar, egg, butter, salt, and mustard; mix well. Bring to a boil. Reduce heat and simmer, stirring constantly, until mixture thickens. Let cool completely.

Combine apple, celery, and chopped walnuts in a large mixing bowl; pour cooled sauce over mixture, mixing well. Cover and refrigerate until thoroughly chilled.

Spoon salad into a serving bowl; garnish with celery leaves and walnut halves, if desired. Yield: 12 servings.

NEW YEAR'S DAY LUNCHEON

The Southern woman is widely known for the grace of her home hospitality. But when she is a member of a group she believes in and works for, she enters wholeheartedly into the "Grand Hotel" form of entertaining. In a given city, women's clubs know for certain which chef at which hotel will carry out their desires and serve a memorable meal. Case in point: In 1929, the Rice Hotel in the center of burgeoning Houston, sponsored a New Year's Day luncheon. The menu, presented here and reduced for home use, was exquisite. The music, besides the house orchestra, included songs by The Virginians and a trio singing "My Cutie's Due At Two To Two."

ESSENCE OF TOMATO SOUP
or
GRAPEFRUIT SALAD SUPREME
STUFFED BREASTS OF CHICKEN
POTATO ROSETTES
CAULIFLOWER WITH HOLLANDAISE
CHILLED ASPARAGUS WITH THOUSAND ISLAND
DRESSING
BISCUIT GLACE AUX MARRONS
DEMITASSE

Serves 6

Gaiety is implicit on menus from the Rice Hotel in Houston.

Harris County Heritage Society

Rice Hotel in Houston, c.1915.

Houston Metropolitan Research Center

GRAPEFRUIT SALAD SUPREME

3 large grapefruit
Romaine, escarole, or chicory
1 cup (4 ounces) shredded
   sharp Cheddar cheese
Golden French Dressing

Cut grapefruit in half crosswise; scoop out pulp, discarding membranes and seeds. Reserve shells and pulp.

Line grapefruit shells with lettuce leaves. Spoon equal amounts of pulp into each shell. Sprinkle equal amounts of cheese over grapefruit. Serve chilled with Golden French Dressing. Yield: 6 servings.

Golden French Dressing:

⅓ cup vegetable oil
⅓ cup lemon juice
1 tablespoon sugar
¼ teaspoon salt
½ teaspoon paprika

Combine all ingredients in a small mixing bowl; mix well. Cover and chill thoroughly. Yield: ⅔ cup.

ESSENCE OF TOMATO SOUP

3 tablespoons chopped onion
3 tablespoons chopped green
   pepper
¼ cup butter or margarine
⅓ cup all-purpose flour
2 (10½-ounce) cans beef
   broth, diluted and divided
1 (14½-ounce) can whole
   tomatoes, undrained and
   chopped
¼ teaspoon salt
¼ teaspoon pepper
Dash of red pepper
1 tablespoon grated fresh
   horseradish
1 teaspoon vinegar

Sauté onion and green pepper in butter in a large saucepan until tender. Combine flour and ½ cup beef broth; stir well. Add flour mixture, remaining broth, and tomatoes to sautéed vegetables; simmer 15 minutes, stirring occasionally. Strain soup, discarding cooked vegetables. Stir in salt and pepper. Cover and refrigerate overnight.

Skim and discard any fat which has risen to the top. Bring soup to a boil over medium heat; stir in horseradish and vinegar. Serve immediately. Yield: 1½ quarts.

STUFFED BREASTS OF CHICKEN

½ cup finely chopped fresh
   mushrooms
2 tablespoons butter or
   margarine
¼ cup plus 2 tablespoons
   all-purpose flour, divided
½ cup half-and-half
1¼ cups (5 ounces) shredded
   sharp Cheddar cheese
¼ teaspoon salt
Dash of pepper
6 chicken breast halves,
   skinned and boned
2 eggs, lightly beaten
1 cup Italian-style fine, dry
   breadcrumbs
Vegetable oil

Sauté mushrooms in butter in a medium skillet. Add 2 tablespoons flour, stirring well. Cook 1 minute, stirring constantly. Gradually add half-and-half; cook over medium heat, stirring constantly, until thickened and bubbly. Add cheese, salt, and pepper, stirring until cheese melts. Remove from heat; cool.

Place each piece of chicken on a sheet of waxed paper; flatten to ¼-inch thickness, using a meat mallot or rolling pin.

Divide cheese mixture into 6 equal portions; roll into logs. Place 1 cheese log in center of each piece of chicken; roll up jellyroll fashion. Tuck in sides. Dredge each roll in ¼ cup flour; dip in egg, and dredge in breadcrumbs. Place rolls in a 12- x 8- x 2-inch baking dish. Cover and refrigerate overnight.

Deep fry rolls in hot oil (375°) just until golden brown. Drain and return rolls to baking dish. Bake at 325° for 30 minutes. Yield: 6 servings.

POTATO ROSETTES

4 medium potatoes, cleaned,
   peeled, and quartered
1 tablespoon butter or
   margarine
½ teaspoon salt
⅛ teaspoon pepper
Dash of paprika
¼ cup whipping cream
1 egg, lightly beaten

Place potatoes with boiling water to cover in a large saucepan; cook 20 minutes or until tender. Drain liquid, reserving potatoes in saucepan; add butter, salt, pepper, and paprika. Mash potatoes until smooth. Add whipping cream; stir well.

Spoon potatoes into a pastry bag fitted with a star tip; pipe onto a lightly greased baking sheet to form 12 rosettes. Brush lightly with beaten egg. Bake at 375° for 20 minutes or until lightly browned. Serve immediately. Yield: 6 servings.

42

The Rice Hotel featured Stuffed Breasts of Chicken in its 1929 men

CAULIFLOWER WITH HOLLANDAISE

1 large head cauliflower
3 egg yolks
½ cup butter or margarine,
 softened and divided
2 tablespoons lemon juice
Dash of hot sauce
¼ teaspoon salt

Wash cauliflower; remove discolorations with a vegetable peeler. Trim stalk, removing core; remove outer leaves. Place cauliflower in a steaming rack over boiling water; cover and steam 10 minutes or until crisp-tender. Drain well; place on a serving plate. Keep warm.

Combine egg yolks and one-third of butter in top of a double boiler. Cook over simmering water, stirring constantly, until butter melts. Add half of remaining butter; stir constantly until butter begins to melt. Add remaining butter, stirring constantly, until butter melts.

Remove pan from water, and stir rapidly 2 minutes. Stir in lemon juice, 1 teaspoon at a time; add hot sauce and salt. Replace over simmering water; cook over low heat, stirring constantly, 2 minutes or until thickened and smooth. Immediately remove from heat, and spoon sauce over cauliflower. Serve warm. Yield: 6 servings.

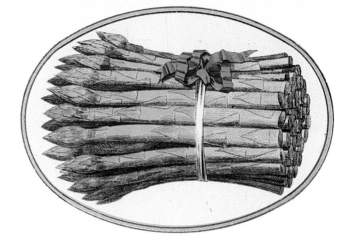

CHILLED ASPARAGUS WITH THOUSAND ISLAND DRESSING

1½ pounds fresh asparagus
 spears
Curly leaf lettuce
Thousand Island Dressing

Snap off tough ends of asparagus. Remove scales from stalks with a knife or vegetable peeler, if desired. Tie asparagus into a bundle with string. Stand bundle, tips up, in bottom of a double boiler. Add boiling water to fill pan half full. Cover with top of double boiler, turned upside down for a lid. Simmer 6 minutes or until asparagus is crisp-tender. Drain and refresh quickly by running asparagus under cold water to retain color; chill thoroughly.

Line a serving dish with lettuce; arrange cut asparagus on top of lettuce. Drizzle Thousand Island Dressing over asparagus, and serve immediately. Yield: 6 servings.

Thousand Island Dressing:

1 cup mayonnaise
¼ cup chili sauce
2 tablespoons vinegar
1 teaspoon paprika
3 hard-cooked eggs, diced
1 small onion, finely chopped
½ cup pimiento-stuffed olives,
 thinly sliced
½ cup finely chopped celery
2 tablespoons minced fresh
 parsley

Combine first four ingredients in a small mixing bowl; stir until well blended. Stir in remaining ingredients. Chill thoroughly. Yield: 2 cups.

BISCUIT GLACE AUX MARRONS

1 cup milk
3 egg yolks
½ cup sugar
1½ teaspoons vanilla extract
1 cup whipping cream
Finely chopped roasted
 chestnuts

Cook milk in top of a double boiler over boiling water, stirring constantly, until milk begins to boil. Remove from heat. Set aside.

Combine egg yolks and sugar in a small mixing bowl, beating until well blended.

Gradually stir one-fourth of reserved milk into egg mixture; add to remaining milk, stirring well. Cook over boiling water, stirring constantly, until mixture coats a metal spoon. Remove from heat; let cool to room temperature. Stir in vanilla. Cover and freeze until slushy.

Beat whipping cream until stiff peaks form. Fold into custard mixture. Spoon mixture into paper-lined muffin pans. Sprinkle evenly with chopped chestnuts. Cover and freeze. Yield: about 1 dozen.

LENTEN LUNCHEON

The complexion of luncheons changes a bit during Lent, although less nowadays than in former years. Along with the dietary restraints of Lent, there used to be a renewed spirit of self-denial and a reaching out to less fortunate folk. Early this century, Lenten parties were frequently combination luncheon-working affairs, to make articles for shut-ins, for example. Charity card parties were held, with each participant anteing up a quarter or half-dollar for the worthy cause; the centerpiece usually went to the nearest hospital. An old-fashioned Lenten luncheon (based on salmon croquettes) can be fun, and we have forty days from which to choose a date.

CREOLE CORN CHOWDER
EGGS AU GRATIN
SALMON CROQUETTES
GREEN PEAS
WHOLE WHEAT ROLLS
HERB BUTTER
LETTUCE WEDGES
WITH ONION SALAD DRESSING
STRAWBERRY SURPRISE

Serves 6

A sewing circle in Augusta, Georgia, c.1910.

Georgia Department of Archives and History

CREOLE CORN CHOWDER

1 medium onion, coarsely chopped
2 green peppers, seeded and chopped
1 tablespoon butter or margarine
4 ears fresh corn, cleaned and cut from cob
2 tomatoes, peeled and chopped
1½ cups water
1½ teaspoons sugar
½ teaspoon salt
¼ teaspoon pepper

Sauté onion and green pepper in butter in a medium saucepan until tender. Add remaining ingredients; bring to a boil. Reduce heat; simmer, uncovered, 1 hour. Serve hot. Yield: about 1¼ quarts.

EGGS AU GRATIN

3 tablespoons butter or margarine
3 tablespoons all-purpose flour
2 cups milk
1¼ cups (5 ounces) shredded sharp Cheddar cheese, divided
½ teaspoon salt
¼ teaspoon pepper
6 eggs

Melt butter in a medium saucepan over low heat; add flour, stirring until smooth. Cook 1 minute, stirring constantly. Gradually add milk; cook over medium heat, stirring constantly, until thickened and bubbly. Add 2 tablespoons cheese, salt, and pepper; stir until cheese melts.

Pour ¼ cup white sauce into six greased 6-ounce custard cups. Break 1 egg into each cup. Cover eggs with remaining sauce; sprinkle remaining cheese evenly over tops.

Place cups in a 13- x 9- x 2-inch baking pan. Cover and bake at 325° for 30 to 35 minutes. Uncover and continue to bake an additional 5 minutes. Serve warm. Yield: 6 servings.

SALMON CROQUETTES

1 (15½-ounce) can pink salmon, drained and flaked
½ teaspoon salt
¼ teaspoon paprika
1 tablespoon butter or margarine
1 tablespoon all-purpose flour
1 cup milk
1 egg
About 3 cups fine, dry breadcrumbs
1 egg, beaten
Vegetable oil
Lemon wedges
Fresh parsley sprigs

Combine salmon, salt, and paprika in a small mixing bowl; stir well, and set aside.

Melt butter in a medium saucepan over low heat; add flour, stirring until smooth. Cook, stirring constantly, 1 minute or until smooth. Gradually add milk; cook over medium heat, stirring constantly, until mixture begins to thicken.

Beat 1 egg until thick and lemon colored. Gradually stir one-fourth of hot mixture into egg; add to remaining hot mixture, stirring constantly. Continue to cook over medium heat, stirring constantly, 1 minute or until thickened. Remove from heat, and stir in reserved salmon mixture. Chill 1 hour.

Shape chilled mixture with floured hands into 12 croquettes; roll each croquette in breadcrumbs, and dip in 1 beaten egg. Roll again in breadcrumbs. Chill several hours.

Cook in deep hot oil (375°) until golden brown. Drain well on paper towels. Transfer croquettes to a serving platter, and garnish with lemon wedges and parsley sprigs. Serve immediately. Yield: 6 servings.

GREEN PEAS

2 pounds fresh green peas (about 4 cups shelled)
1 teaspoon salt
1 tablespoon butter or margarine
½ teaspoon pepper
Pimiento strips (optional)

Snap off top of each pea pod, and pull string down side of pod. Remove peas; rinse shelled peas in cold water; drain.

Fill a small Dutch oven half full of water; add salt, and bring to a rolling boil. Add shelled peas; return to a boil. Reduce heat; cover and simmer 25 minutes or until peas are tender. Drain well.

Transfer to a serving bowl; season with butter and pepper. Garnish with pimiento strips, if desired. Yield: 6 servings.

Turn-of-the-century green peas label.

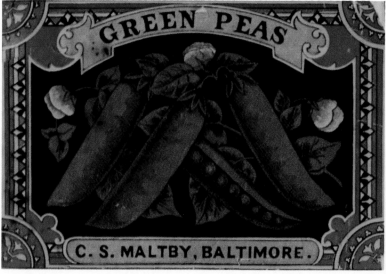

WHOLE WHEAT ROLLS

1 package dry yeast
½ cup warm water (105° to 115°), divided
½ cup milk, scalded
2 tablespoons butter or margarine
2 tablespoons honey
1½ teaspoons salt
1 cup all-purpose flour
2 cups whole wheat flour
1 tablespoon butter or margarine, melted

Dissolve yeast in 2 tablespoons water; let stand 5 minutes. Combine milk, 2 tablespoons butter, honey, salt, and remaining water in a medium mixing bowl; mix well. Cool. Add dissolved yeast; mix well. Gradually stir in flour.

Turn dough out onto a lightly floured surface, and knead 10 minutes or until smooth and elastic. Place dough in a well-greased bowl, turning to grease top. Cover and let rise in a warm place (85°), free from drafts, 1 hour or until doubled in bulk.

Punch dough down, and turn out onto a floured surface. Divide into 12 equal portions. Shape each portion into a ball, and place 2 inches apart on a greased baking sheet. Brush with melted butter. Cover and repeat rising procedure 45 minutes or until doubled in bulk. Bake at 350° for 18 minutes or until lightly browned. Yield: 1 dozen.

HERB BUTTER

1 cup butter, softened
1 tablespoon minced fresh parsley
1 small clove garlic, minced
¼ teaspoon finely chopped fresh thyme

Cream butter in a small mixing bowl. Stir in remaining ingredients. Refrigerate and store in a covered container until ready to use. Let butter soften before serving with Whole Wheat Rolls. Yield: about 1 cup.

To satisfy, offer Creole Corn Chowder and Whole Wheat Rolls with Herb Butter.

LETTUCE WEDGES WITH ONION SALAD DRESSING

Lettuce wedges
1 cup mayonnaise
½ cup vegetable oil
¼ cup chili sauce
¼ cup catsup
2 tablespoons water
1 tablespoon vinegar
1 tablespoon Worcestershire sauce
1 teaspoon prepared mustard
½ teaspoon salt
½ teaspoon pepper
⅛ teaspoon paprika
1 tablespoon grated onion
2 cloves garlic, minced

Combine all ingredients, except lettuce. Cover and refrigerate. Serve over lettuce wedges. Yield: 2 cups.

STRAWBERRY SURPRISE

1 quart fresh strawberries, washed, hulled, and pureed
4 egg whites
2 cups sugar
1 cup water

Combine all ingredients in freezer can of a 1-gallon hand-turned or electric freezer; stir well. Freeze according to manufacturer's instructions. Let ripen at least 1 hour. Scoop into individual dessert bowls to serve. Yield: 3 quarts.

POLK PILGRIMAGE LUNCHEON

Women's groups in the South have helped save countless shrines from oblivion. The home of President James K. Polk's parents in Columbia, Tennessee, is one such treasure. The building, built in 1816, was purchased in 1929 by the Polk Memorial Association. The Columbia Auxiliary of the Association oversees its operation and every April serves a luncheon to 200 people. Their recipes follow.

SWEET AND SOUR PICKLES
SPINACH SOUFFLÉ WITH MUSHROOM SAUCE
CHEESE STICKS
SPICY TOMATO ASPIC
or
SLICED TOMATOES
TURKEY SALAD
POTATO ROLLS
SWISS CHOCOLATE TARTS
TEA

Serves 12

SWEET AND SOUR PICKLES

4 (16-ounce) jars whole sour pickles
½ (1.25-ounce) package mixed pickling spices
5 cups sugar, divided
1 clove garlic, minced and divided
½ cup vinegar (5% acidity)

Drain pickles, discarding liquid and reserving jars. Cut pickles into ¼-inch-thick slices. Tie pickling spices in cheesecloth. Place half of pickles in a large crock or plastic container; add spice bag. Sprinkle half the sugar and garlic over pickles; repeat layers of pickles, sugar, and garlic. Pour vinegar over mixture. Cover and let stand in a cool place 24 hours. Stir mixture well; cover and let stand another 24 hours.

Remove spice bag. Return pickles to jars, and refrigerate until ready to use. Yield: 12 servings.

SPINACH SOUFFLÉ WITH MUSHROOM SAUCE

12 slices bread, crust removed
½ cup butter or margarine, melted
3 cups milk, divided
6 eggs
2 (10-ounce) packages frozen spinach, thawed and drained
1½ teaspoons Worcestershire sauce
1 teaspoon salt
¾ teaspoon dry mustard
2 cups (8 ounces) shredded sharp Cheddar cheese
1 cup (4 ounces) shredded Swiss cheese
1 teaspoon grated onion
½ cup grated Parmesan cheese
Mushroom Sauce

Spread bread slices with melted butter; place bread in a large bowl, and set aside.

Combine 1 cup milk, eggs, spinach, Worcestershire sauce, salt, and mustard in container of an electric blender; process until well blended. Pour egg mixture and remaining milk over bread; let stand 5 minutes.

Stir with a wire whisk until well blended. Stir in Cheddar and Swiss cheese and onion.

Pour mixture into a greased 13- x 9- x 2-inch baking dish. Bake, uncovered, at 350° for 50 minutes; sprinkle top with Parmesan cheese, and continue baking 10 minutes or until set. Let stand 10 minutes; score into 3- x 3-inch squares. Serve with Mushroom Sauce. Yield: 12 servings.

Mushroom Sauce:

¼ cup plus 2 tablespoons butter or margarine
¼ cup plus 2 tablespoons cake flour
2¼ cups chicken broth
1½ cups milk
½ teaspoon salt
⅛ teaspoon pepper
1 (6-ounce) jar sliced mushrooms, drained

Melt butter in a large heavy saucepan over low heat. Add flour; stir until smooth. Cook 1 minute, stirring constantly. Gradually add chicken broth and milk; cook over medium heat, stirring constantly, until thickened and bubbly. Stir in salt, pepper, and mushrooms. Serve warm. Yield: 1 quart.

CHEESE STICKS

1 cup (4 ounces) shredded
  New York State Cheddar
  cheese
½ cup butter or margarine,
  softened
1¾ cups sifted cake flour
¼ teaspoon salt
¼ teaspoon red pepper

Combine cheese and butter in a large mixing bowl; mix well. Set aside.

Combine flour, salt, and red pepper in a small mixing bowl; stir well. Gradually add flour mixture to cheese mixture, mixing until dough is no longer crumbly. Shape dough into a ball. Divide dough in half; roll each half into a rectangle ⅓-inch thick on waxed paper. Use a pastry wheel to cut dough into 4- x ½-inch strips.

Place strips on greased baking sheets. Bake at 350° for 20 minutes. Remove to wire racks to cool. Store sticks in airtight containers, placing waxed paper between layers. Yield: about 4 dozen.

SPICY TOMATO ASPIC

3 packages unflavored gelatin
5½ cups tomato juice, divided
⅓ cup lemon juice
1 tablespoon grated onion
1 clove garlic, minced
1 teaspoon dillweed or
  dillseeds
½ teaspoon dried whole basil
½ teaspoon dried whole
  oregano
1 small bay leaf, crushed
Lettuce leaves
Fresh parsley sprigs
Lemon twists

Soften gelatin in ½ cup tomato juice; set aside.

Combine remaining tomato juice and next 7 ingredients in a large saucepan; bring to a boil. Reduce heat, and simmer 10 minutes. Strain tomato juice mixture; add gelatin mixture, stirring until gelatin dissolves. Pour into a lightly oiled 5½-cup ring mold; chill until set.

Turn mold out onto a lettuce-lined serving plate, and garnish with parsley and lemon twists. Yield: 12 servings.

TURKEY SALAD

4 cups chopped, cooked
  turkey
2 hard-cooked eggs, chopped
1 cup pickle relish
¼ cup finely chopped onion
1 cup mayonnaise
2 tablespoons prepared
  mustard
2 teaspoons celery seeds
½ teaspoon salt
½ teaspoon paprika
¼ teaspoon pepper
Lettuce leaves

Combine turkey, egg, pickle relish, and onion. Combine mayonnaise and seasonings, stirring until well blended; add to turkey mixture, mixing well. Chill. Serve on lettuce leaves with Tomato Aspic, if desired. Yield: 12 servings.

Note: Turkey Salad may be served in center of Tomato Aspic, if desired.

Spinach Soufflé, the perfect dish for your next buffet, can be multiplied as needed.

POTATO ROLLS

1 package dry yeast
½ cup sugar, divided
¼ cup warm water (105° to 115°)
2 cups milk, scalded
1¾ cups mashed, cooked potatoes
3 tablespoons lard or shortening
2 teaspoons salt
1 egg, lightly beaten
6 to 7 cups all-purpose flour, divided

Dissolve yeast and 1 teaspoon sugar in warm water, stirring well. Let stand 5 minutes or until bubbly.

Combine milk, potatoes, lard, and salt in a large mixing bowl; stir until lard melts. Add yeast mixture and egg, stirring until well blended. Add 3½ cups flour, stirring well. Cover and let rise in a warm place (85°), free from drafts, 1 hour or until doubled in bulk. Add enough remaining flour to make a soft dough.

Place dough in a lightly greased bowl, turning to grease top. Cover and refrigerate overnight.

Roll dough to ½-inch thickness on a lightly floured surface; cut with a 2½-inch biscuit cutter. Place rolls on lightly greased baking sheets; cover and repeat rising procedure 45 minutes or until doubled in bulk. Bake at 400° for 10 to 12 minutes. Serve warm. Yield: about 5½ dozen.

G.P.A. Healy's portrait of Sarah Childress Polk, 1846.

Home of President James K. Polk

SWISS CHOCOLATE TARTS

½ cup sugar
¼ cup cake flour
¼ teaspoon salt
1 cup milk
1 (1-ounce) square unsweetened chocolate
1 tablespoon butter or margarine
6 large marshmallows
Hot Water Tart Shells
1 cup whipping cream, whipped
Grated mint chocolate

Combine sugar, flour, and salt in top of a double boiler. Add milk, stirring constantly. Cook over boiling water, stirring constantly, until mixture thickens. Melt chocolate square and butter in a small saucepan over low heat; add to milk mixture; stir. Add marshmallows. Stir until marshmallows melt and mixture is smooth. Remove from heat, and cool completely. Spoon chocolate mixture evenly into tart shells.

Beat whipping cream until stiff peaks form. Place a dollop of whipped cream on each tart. Sprinkle with mint chocolate. Serve cold. Yield: 1 dozen.

Hot Water Tart Shells:

¾ cup all-purpose flour
¼ teaspoon baking powder
¼ teaspoon salt
¼ cup shortening
2 tablespoons boiling water

Combine flour, baking powder, and salt in a small mixing bowl; cut in shortening with a pastry blender until mixture resembles coarse meal. Sprinkle boiling water over surface; stir with a fork until dry ingredients are moistened. Shape dough into a ball; chill overnight.

Divide dough into 12 equal portions. Roll each portion to ⅛-inch thickness on a lightly floured surface. Fit each pastry into a 3-inch tart pan or 2¾-inch muffin pan. Prick bottom and sides of tart shells with a fork. Bake at 350° for 12 to 15 minutes. Cool in pan on a wire rack. Yield: 1 dozen tart shells.

RIVER OAKS GARDEN CLUB LUNCHEON

In October of 1927, three women met at the home of Mrs. A. C. Bayless of River Oaks to organize a garden club. Their first project was to create a wildflower garden; their dues were $1 a year. They ended the first year with $8.44 in the bank and spent it on garden manuals for members to study. Ima Hogg, a member, gave up rights to *A Garden Book for Houston* to benefit the club. When the club celebrated its golden anniversary in 1977, five of the original members attended. For 50 years, the River Oaks Club has sponsored the Azalea Trail, the pride of Houston. This is the luncheon (a 1942 menu) prepared by members for the hostesses of the homes on tour.

CREAM OF SPINACH SOUP
CHICKEN-ALMOND SANDWICHES
ROLLED ASPARAGUS SANDWICHES
DOMINO SANDWICHES
CUCUMBER AND WATERCRESS SANDWICHES
CREAM CHEESE AND PINEAPPLE SANDWICHES
DEVILED EGGS WITH ANCHOVIES
WATERMELON RIND PICKLES
GINGERBREAD WITH LEMON SAUCE
SOUR CREAM-COCOA CAKE

Serves 12

CREAM OF SPINACH SOUP

1 small onion, coarsely chopped
3 tablespoons butter or margarine
3 tablespoons all-purpose flour
2 cups milk
½ teaspoon salt
¼ teaspoon pepper
Dash of red pepper
Dash of ground nutmeg
2 cups cooked and drained spinach
1 cup diluted beef consommé
2 cups half-and-half
⅓ cup sherry

Sauté onion in butter in a large Dutch oven until tender; remove onion with a slotted spoon. Drain well, and set aside.

Add flour to butter, stirring until smooth. Cook over low heat 1 minute, stirring constantly. Gradually add milk; cook over medium heat, stirring constantly, until thickened and bubbly. Stir in salt, pepper, and nutmeg.

Process spinach, consommé, and sautéed onion in container of an electric blender until smooth. Add to white sauce, stirring well. Stir in half-and-half. Cook until thoroughly heated. (Do not boil.) Stir in sherry just before serving. Serve warm. Yield: 3 quarts.

CHICKEN-ALMOND SANDWICHES

1 cup diced, cooked chicken
1 cup chopped almonds
¼ cup chopped celery
½ cup mayonnaise
2 tablespoons plus 2 teaspoons half-and-half
¼ teaspoon salt
¼ teaspoon pepper
¼ teaspoon paprika
24 slices white bread, crust removed
2 tablespoons butter or margarine, softened

Combine first 8 ingredients; mix well. Cut bread into matching shapes, and spread with butter. Spread chicken mixture evenly on half of bread shapes; top with remaining bread shapes. Yield: about 2 dozen.

ROLLED ASPARAGUS SANDWICHES

12 fresh asparagus spears
¼ cup mayonnaise
1½ teaspoons honey
½ teaspoon lime juice
⅛ teaspoon curry powder
12 slices white bread, crust removed
Carrot strips (optional)

Snap off tough ends of asparagus, leaving a 4½-inch tip; discard ends. Fill a saucepan three-fourths full with salted water; bring to a boil. Place asparagus in boiling water; cover and cook until water returns to a boil. Reduce heat; simmer, uncovered, 12 minutes or until a knife point will easily pierce tips. Drain; cover and chill.

Combine mayonnaise, honey, lime juice, and curry powder in a small mixing bowl; mix well.

Flatten each slice of bread, using a rolling pin. Spread each slice with mayonnaise mixture; place 1 asparagus spear on each, and roll up jellyroll fashion. Garnish with carrot strips, if desired. Yield: 1 dozen.

DOMINO SANDWICHES

1 cup finely chopped, cooked ham
3 tablespoons mayonnaise
1 small dill pickle, minced
1 tablespoon butter or margarine, softened
4 slices thin-sliced whole wheat bread, crust removed
4 slices thin-sliced white bread, crust removed
3 (⅔-ounce) slices Swiss cheese

Combine ham, mayonnaise, and minced pickle in a small mixing bowl; mix well.

Spread softened butter evenly on each bread slice. Spread ham mixture on one slice of white bread; top with a slice of wheat bread. Place 1 cheese slice on top of wheat bread. Repeat layers with remaining ingredients to form a tall stack.

Wrap sandwich in waxed paper; put under a weight, and chill. Cut lengthwise into 3 rectangles; cut each rectangle into fourths. Yield: 1 dozen.

Mike, Ima, and Tom Hogg, 1903. Miss Hogg donated her talent to the River Oaks Club.

CUCUMBER AND WATERCRESS SANDWICHES

1 medium cucumber, peeled and thinly sliced
½ cup vinegar
½ cup water
6 ice cubes
½ teaspoon dried whole dillweed
½ teaspoon salt
¼ teaspoon pepper
12 slices white bread
1 tablespoon butter or margarine, softened
Watercress leaves

Combine cucumber, vinegar, water, and ice cubes in a small mixing bowl; let stand 30 minutes. Drain well.

Sprinkle dillweed, salt, and pepper over cucumber; toss gently.

Remove crust from bread; cut 2 rounds from each slice, using a 2-inch cutter. (Cut larger or smaller, depending on diameter of cucumber.) Spread softened butter over each round; place a slice of cucumber on each. Garnish each with watercress. Yield: 2 dozen.

Note: Whole wheat bread may be used instead of white bread.

CREAM CHEESE AND PINEAPPLE SANDWICHES

2 (3-ounce) packages cream cheese, softened
½ cup crushed pineapple, drained
½ cup chopped pecans
5 slices thin-sliced whole wheat bread, crust removed
2 tablespoons butter or margarine, softened
Pineapple tidbits (optional)

Combine cream cheese, crushed pineapple, and pecans in a small mixing bowl; stir well.

Spread softened butter on each bread slice. Spread cream cheese mixture on one side of bread; cut each into 3 rectangles. Garnish with pineapple tidbits, if desired. Yield: about 1½ dozen.

DEVILED EGGS WITH ANCHOVIES

1 dozen hard-cooked eggs
¼ cup salad dressing
2 tablespoons tarragon vinegar
1 teaspoon dry mustard
¼ teaspoon salt
1 (2-ounce) can anchovies, cut into small pieces
Paprika
Fresh parsley sprigs

Slice eggs in half lengthwise, and carefully remove yolks. Place yolks in a small mixing bowl, and mash. Stir in salad dressing, vinegar, mustard, and salt, mixing well.

Stuff egg whites with yolk mixture. Sprinkle anchovies evenly over deviled eggs. Sprinkle with paprika, and garnish with parsley. Chill 3 hours. Yield: 12 servings.

Note: Egg yolk mixture may be spooned into a pastry bag fitted with a star tip and piped into hard-cooked whites.

The River Oaks Garden Club luncheon is one of the most spectacular of such offerings in the South.

Barker Texas History Center, University of Texas at Austin

WATERMELON RIND PICKLES

1 medium watermelon, quartered
5⅓ cups water
1 teaspoon salt
½ teaspoon alum
½ teaspoon flaked mace
¾ teaspoon whole cloves
1 (3-inch) stick cinnamon, broken into pieces
1⅓ cups vinegar
4 cups sugar

Peel watermelon; remove flesh. Cut rind into 1-inch cubes.

Combine rind, water, salt, and alum in a large Dutch oven; bring to a boil. Reduce heat; simmer, uncovered, 10 minutes. Drain, discarding liquid. Place rind in ice water to cover; let stand 30 minutes. Drain; place rind in a large crock or plastic container.

Tie mace, cloves, and cinnamon in cheesecloth. Combine spice bag, vinegar, and sugar in a large non-aluminum saucepan; bring to a boil. Pour hot syrup over rind to cover. Add spice bag. Cover and refrigerate overnight.

Drain syrup from rind into a medium non-aluminum saucepan; set rind aside. Bring syrup to a boil. Pour hot syrup over spice bag and rind; stir well. Cover and refrigerate overnight. Repeat procedure for 7 days.

On the eighth day, drain syrup into a large non-aluminum saucepan; set rind aside. Bring syrup to a boil; add rind, discarding spice bag. Return to a boil. Reduce heat; simmer, uncovered, 10 minutes.

Pack rind into hot sterilized jars, leaving a ½-inch headspace; pour hot syrup over rind, leaving a ¼-inch headspace. Remove air bubbles, stirring with the handle of a wooden spoon. Cover at once with metal lids, and screw bands tight. Process in boiling-water bath 5 minutes. Yield: about 3 pints.

GINGERBREAD WITH LEMON SAUCE

1 cup butter or margarine, softened
1 cup sugar
4 eggs
1 cup molasses
4 cups all-purpose flour
1 teaspoon ground cinnamon
2 teaspoons ground ginger
½ teaspoon ground allspice
½ teaspoon ground nutmeg
2 teaspoons baking soda
1 cup buttermilk
Lemon Sauce

Cream butter in a large mixing bowl; gradually add sugar, beating until light and fluffy. Add eggs, one at a time, beating well after each addition. Add molasses; beat well.

Sift together flour and spices in a medium mixing bowl.

Dissolve soda in buttermilk. Add flour mixture to creamed mixture alternately with buttermilk mixture, beginning and ending with flour mixture.

Pour batter into a well-greased 13- x 9- x 2-inch baking pan. Bake at 350° for 40 to 45 minutes. Cool in pan 10 minutes; cut into squares. Serve warm with Lemon Sauce. Yield: 12 servings.

Lemon Sauce:

¾ cup water
½ cup sugar
2 teaspoons all-purpose flour
1 egg, well beaten
Grated rind and juice of 1 lemon
½ cup whipping cream, whipped

Combine water, sugar, and flour in a small saucepan. Cook over medium heat, stirring constanty, until slightly thickened. Remove from heat.

Gradually stir one-fourth of hot mixture into beaten egg in a small mixing bowl; add to remaining hot mixture. Return to low heat; cook, stirring constantly, until thickened and smooth. Cool slightly; stir in lemon rind and juice. Cool completely; fold in whipped cream. Serve chilled. Yield: 2 cups.

SOUR CREAM-COCOA CAKE

½ cup cocoa
¾ cup boiling water
½ cup shortening
2 cups sugar
2 cups cake flour
½ teaspoon baking soda
½ teaspoon salt
½ cup sour cream
1 teaspoon vanilla extract
3 egg whites
Mocha Frosting
3 tablespoons chopped pecans

Combine cocoa and boiling water; stir until smooth. Cool to room temperature.

Cream shortening; gradually add sugar, beating well. Stir in cooled cocoa mixture.

Sift together flour, soda, and salt; add to creamed mixture alternately with sour cream, beginning and ending with flour mixture. Stir in vanilla.

Beat egg whites (at room temperature) until stiff peaks form. Fold egg whites into batter. Pour batter evenly into 2 greased and waxed paper-lined 8-inch square cakepans. Bake at 350° for 40 minutes or until a wooden pick inserted in center comes out clean. Cool in pans 10 minutes; remove layers from pans, and cool completely on wire racks.

Spread Mocha Frosting evenly between layers and on top and sides of cooled cake. Sprinkle top with pecans. Yield: one 2-layer cake.

Mocha Frosting:

¼ cup plus 2 tablespoons butter or margarine, softened
4 cups sifted powdered sugar
3 tablespoons brewed coffee, chilled

Cream butter; gradually add sugar, beating well. Add coffee, and beat until smooth. Yield: frosting for one 2-layer cake.

HARVEST LUNCHEON

ven today, generations after the American pumpkin appeared in pureed and tinned form for use the year round, practically all the pumpkin that is used in the United States is used primarily during harvesttime. For an autumn luncheon, the only decision to be made is whether to put pumpkin in the soup, the bread, or in one of the luscious desserts found in the Southern repertoire. Today's decision is muffins. And to complement them is an array of good things to eat. This comfortable luncheon starts with a perky bisque and ends with another harvesttime treat — apples, stuffed with a spicy mixture and baked in orange juice.

CREAM OF BROCCOLI SOUP
DILLED GREEN OLIVES
NORMANDY LUNCHEON SALAD
CHEDDAR CHEESE LOG
DEVILED WAFERS
PUMPKIN MUFFINS
HARVEST BAKED APPLES

Serves 8

News photo of a luncheon in Murphy, North Carolina, numbered to identify guests, c.1910.

CREAM OF BROCCOLI SOUP

3 (10-ounce) packages chopped frozen broccoli
½ cup plus 1 tablespoon butter or margarine
¾ cup all-purpose flour
3 cups milk
1½ teaspoons salt
2 cups (8 ounces) shredded sharp Cheddar cheese
¾ cup beer
Seasoned croutons

Cook broccoli according to package directions; do not drain. Place broccoli and cooking liquid in container of an electric blender; process until smooth. Set aside.

Melt butter in a small Dutch oven over low heat; add flour, stirring until smooth. Cook 1 minute, stirring constantly. Gradually add milk; cook over medium heat, stirring constantly, until thickened and bubbly. Stir in salt. Add cheese; stir constantly until cheese melts and mixture is smooth. Stir in pureed broccoli and beer. Cook over medium heat until thoroughly heated.

Serve hot in individual serving bowls; sprinkle with seasoned croutons. Yield: about 2 quarts.

DILLED GREEN OLIVES

1 (10-ounce) jar jumbo green olives
½ cup olive oil
¼ cup vinegar
2 tablespoons minced fresh dill
1 clove garlic, sliced
1 slice hot red pepper, seeded
¼ teaspoon pepper

Drain olives, reserving jar and discarding liquid. Return olives to jar; set aside.

Combine remaining ingredients in a small saucepan. Bring to a boil, and cook 3 minutes. Remove from heat; cool slightly. Pour mixture into jar; cover and refrigerate overnight. Yield: 8 servings.

NORMANDY LUNCHEON SALAD

1 large head iceberg lettuce, torn
4 medium tomatoes, cut into wedges
2 large green peppers, seeded and cut into ¼-inch strips
1 large cucumber, peeled and sliced
1 medium onion, sliced
5 radish roses
1 cup diagonally sliced celery
¾ pound thinly sliced cooked ham, cut into 2-inch strips
¾ pound thinly sliced cooked chicken or turkey, cut into 2-inch strips
4 hard-cooked eggs, sliced
Salad dressing (recipe follows)

Combine vegetables in a large bowl; toss well. Arrange ham, chicken, and eggs on salad. Serve with salad dressing. Yield: 8 servings.

Salad Dressing:

1½ cups vegetable oil
⅔ cup red wine vinegar
2 teaspoons catsup
2 small cloves garlic, minced
2 teaspoons minced onion
1 teaspoon sugar
1 teaspoon salt
1 teaspoon pepper

Combine all ingredients in a jar. Cover tightly, and shake vigorously. Chill thoroughly. Yield: 2¼ cups.

Normandy Luncheon Salad, Cheddar Cheese Log, and Deviled Wafers: part of a harmonious lunch menu.

Fresh jack-o-lanterns take form right in the field, as children prepare for a happy Halloween.

CHEDDAR CHEESE LOG

1 pound sharp Cheddar cheese
1 tablespoon grated onion
1 teaspoon Worcestershire sauce
½ teaspoon paprika
½ cup finely chopped pecans
Cheese flowers (optional)
Ripe olive slices (optional)
Pimiento slices (optional)

Dice cheese into small pieces, and let stand until room temperature. Place cheese in a large mixing bowl; beat at medium speed of an electric mixer until cheese is smooth and creamy. Add onion, Worcestershire sauce, and paprika, beating until well blended. Shape cheese into a long roll, 2 inches in diameter. Roll log in pecans until log is well coated, and wrap in waxed paper. Chill overnight or until firm.

Let log stand 10 minutes. Garnish with cheese flowers, olive slices, and pimiento strips, if desired. Serve with Deviled Wafers. Yield: one 12-inch long cheese log.

Note: Make cheese flowers, using a canapé cutter.

DEVILED WAFERS

½ cup butter or margarine
1 teaspoon Worcestershire sauce
5 dozen saltine crackers
Paprika

Cream butter in a small mixing bowl; add Worcestershire sauce, mixing well.

Spread crackers lightly with creamed mixture. Sprinkle with paprika. Place crackers on a 15- x 10- x 1-inch jellyroll pan. Bake at 350° for 5 minutes. Yield: 5 dozen.

PUMPKIN MUFFINS

½ cup raisins
1 cup all-purpose flour, divided
¾ cup sugar, divided
2 teaspoons baking powder
¼ teaspoon salt
½ teaspoon ground cinnamon
½ teaspoon ground nutmeg
¼ cup butter or margarine, softened
1 egg, well beaten
½ cup mashed, cooked pumpkin
½ cup evaporated milk

Combine raisins and 1 tablespoon flour; stir well. Set aside.

Sift together remaining flour, ½ cup sugar, baking powder, salt, cinnamon, and nutmeg. Cut in butter with a pastry blender until mixture resembles coarse meal. Make a well in center of mixture. Combine egg, pumpkin, and milk; add to dry ingredients, stirring just until dry ingredients are moistened. Stir in reserved raisin mixture.

Spoon batter into greased muffin pans, filling two-thirds full. Sprinkle remaining sugar evenly over muffins. Bake at 400° for 20 to 25 minutes. Yield: 1 dozen.

HARVEST BAKED APPLES

8 medium-size cooking apples, cored
¾ cup raisins
¼ cup all-purpose flour
⅓ cup plus 2 tablespoons sugar
¾ teaspoon ground cinnamon
¼ cup butter or margarine, softened
⅓ cup finely chopped pecans
¾ cup orange juice
¾ cup water
1 cup whipping cream, whipped

Place apples in a greased 13- x 9- x 2-inch baking dish. Stuff each apple equally with raisins. Set aside.

Combine flour, sugar, and cinnamon in a small mixing bowl; stir well. Cut in butter with a pastry blender until mixture resembles coarse meal; stir in pecans. Stuff pecan mixture equally in centers of apples. Pour orange juice and water in bottom of dish.

Bake at 375° for 1 hour or until apples are tender, basting often. Garnish each apple with a dollop of whipped cream. Serve immediately. Yield: 8 servings.

THE PLEASURE OF YOUR COMPANY

The pleasure belongs to the guests when served Champagne Punch and Hot Russian Tea to accompany Cheese Straws, Baked Ham Sandwiches, and Date Roll Sandwiches.

The South was probably the last region of the country to give up hand-delivered invitations; some may remember the first mailed invitation their mothers received. And long after the telephone became a household fixture, it was, nevertheless, shunned in favor of engraved invitations if the social function were consequential. Given the easygoing ways into which we have fallen, we can only guess at how it must have felt to have answered a rap on the door and have had a messenger hand us an invitation. Luncheons, teas, receptions, dinners — all social affairs implying dignity and formality still require invitations on the finest paper, mailed well in advance.

Teas, for as long as any of us remembers, have been among the most pleasurable parties of leisure. We learned to like tea from our English settlers, though tea as a breakfast beverage has been superseded by coffee in most circles. To talk of tea parties, though, we must go back to the English difference between high tea and low or afternoon tea. Contrary to most people's conception, high tea originated with the working classes and was a fairly substantial 6 o'clock meal with meat pies and hearty breads. Low tea, between two and six, was customary in well-to-do families, requiring the best china and linens and dainty foods. A large stand-up tea features finger foods and an additional beverage or two.

The people whose parties are remembered in this chapter include not only important public figures, but also women who shone forth in their day as gracious hostesses. And how they parlayed their party-giving skills into civic accomplishments is a story in itself. Men not only attended and loved the teas and receptions, they also gave such entertainments themselves, calling on women friends to arrange the flowers and pour the tea and punch.

We may easily succumb to nostalgia on reading of the social scene during and before Grandmother's day unless we realize that most such entertaining can still be done — with a difference, of course. On a golden day, we can extend our home to porch, veranda, lawn, or garden and invite as many people as we please for a tea or a reception.

MRS. McCREA RECEIVES
AT CARTER'S GROVE

When Archibald and Mary Corling McCrea bought Carter's Grove in 1927, it was in such disrepair that it took three years to restore. Mrs. McCrea, related to several of Virginia's first families, referred to "The Grove," situated on the James River in Williamsburg, as the child of her old age. By 1930 the renowned hostess had restored Carter's Grove to its former grandeur as a social center; persons of international prominence were again being entertained there. In what has been described as the most beautiful house in America, Mrs. McCrea received 300 guests when the French Official Delegation came to Virginia for the Yorktown Sesquicentennial in 1931.

BAKED HAM SANDWICHES
DATE ROLL SANDWICHES
CHEESE STRAWS
CHAMPAGNE PUNCH
RUSSIAN TEA

Serves 24

BAKED HAM SANDWICHES

12 slices thin-sliced white bread, crust removed
12 slices thin-sliced whole wheat bread, crust removed
12 slices thin-sliced rye bread, crust removed
⅓ cup mayonnaise
⅓ cup prepared mustard
1 pound baked ham, thinly sliced
1 (16-ounce) jar dill pickle slices
Fresh parsley sprigs

Combine mayonnaise and mustard in a small mixing bowl, blending well. Spread mayonnaise mixture evenly on one side of each bread slice.

Arrange a ham slice on 6 slices of each variety of bread; place several pickle slices on top of ham. Top with remaining bread slices, mayonnaise side down, matching bread varieties. Cut each sandwich into four triangles. Arrange sandwiches on a serving platter, and garnish with parsley. Yield: 6 dozen.

Note: An onion slice may be placed on top of pickle.

Mrs. Archibald McCrea at Carter's Grove, c.1931.

DATE ROLL SANDWICHES

1 cup sugar
2 eggs
⅔ cup molasses
¼ cup shortening, melted
1½ cups all-purpose flour
1½ cups whole wheat flour
1 teaspoon baking soda
1 teaspoon salt
1 (8-ounce) package
  chopped dates
1 cup chopped raisins
1 cup buttermilk
2 (8-ounce) packages cream
  cheese, softened

Combine sugar and eggs in a large mixing bowl; beat at medium speed of an electric mixer until well blended. Add molasses and melted shortening, beating well; set aside.

Sift together flour, soda, and salt; dredge dates and raisins in ⅓ cup flour mixture, and set aside. Gradually add remaining flour mixture to reserved molasses mixture alternately with buttermilk, beginning and ending with flour mixture. Beat well after each addition. Fold in reserved date-raisin mixture.

Pour 1 cup batter into each of seven well-greased 10¾-ounce soup cans. Bake at 325° for 1 hour and 10 minutes or until a wooden pick inserted in center comes out clean.

Cool 10 minutes in cans on wire racks. Remove loaves from cans, and cool completely on wire racks. Cut each loaf into 12 slices. Spread cream cheese evenly over half of date bread slices; top with remaining slices. Cut each sandwich in half. Arrange sandwiches on a serving platter. Yield: 7 dozen sandwiches.

Hot Russian Tea, flavored with citrus and spices, is a lovely reception offering. The teapot is in the elegant Repoussé pattern.

CHEESE STRAWS

2 cups (8 ounces) shredded
  sharp Cheddar cheese
½ cup butter or margarine,
  softened
1½ cups all-purpose flour
½ teaspoon salt
½ to ¾ teaspoon red pepper

Combine cheese and butter in a large mixing bowl; mix well. Set aside.

Combine flour, salt, and pepper in a medium mixing bowl; mix well. Gradually add to cheese mixture, stirring until dough is no longer crumbly. Form dough into a ball. (Bowl may be placed in warm water until dough is soft enough to form a ball.)

Use a cookie press fitted with a star disc to shape dough into straws. Place straws on greased baking sheets. Bake at 350° for 10 minutes or until lightly browned. Store straws in airtight containers, placing waxed paper between layers. Yield: 5 dozen.

CHAMPAGNE PUNCH

2 cups lemon juice
1½ cups sugar
2 (750 ml) bottles Sauterne,
  chilled
2 (750 ml) bottles champagne,
  chilled
Ice ring (optional)
Lemon slices (optional)

Combine lemon juice and sugar in a small non-aluminum saucepan. Bring to a boil; cook, stirring constantly, until sugar dissolves. Chill thoroughly.

Pour lemon juice mixture into a punch bowl just before serving. Gently pour in Sauterne and champagne. Add ice ring and garnish with lemon slices, if desired. Serve immediately. Yield: about 2½ quarts.

RUSSIAN TEA

8 oranges, sliced
6 lemons, sliced
6 (3-inch) sticks cinnamon
1 tablespoon whole
  cloves
1 quart water
1 (46-ounce) can pineapple
  juice
1½ cups sugar
3 quarts tea

Combine fruit slices, cinnamon, cloves, and water in a large non-aluminum saucepan; bring to a boil. Boil 5 minutes. Press mixture through a strainer, discarding pulp and spices. Add pineapple juice, sugar, and tea to citrus mixture, stirring well. Serve hot. Yield: about 2 gallons.

AT HOME IN HOUSTON

Houston grew rapidly after 1901, when the oil gushed forth, but the city's origin coincides with its independence from Mexico in 1836. The Harris County (Texas) Heritage Society counts Mrs. Charles William Robertson among its most important early Houstonians. When she came there as a young matron and wife of a cotton magnate, she brought with her the English "at home" custom of receiving friends on a designated day of the week. In her case it was Wednesday, and her chosen costume varied little: with a soft black dress, she wore a black "dog collar" of jet beads and a string of pearls. Most important to her was the conversation, so she chose her guests carefully. She used a standardized menu: dainty sandwiches, Sand Tarts, and tea.

CELERY-NUT SANDWICHES
CHUTNEY SANDWICHES
SAND TARTS
CHOCOLATE CREAM DROPS
SPICED RUM TEA

Serves 8 to 10

Chutney Sandwiches with cream cheese go on a party plate with Celery-Nut Sandwiches: a nice twosome.

CELERY-NUT SANDWICHES

1 cup finely chopped celery
½ cup finely chopped pecans
¼ cup mayonnaise
Additional mayonnaise
36 slices thin-sliced whole wheat bread

Combine celery, pecans, and ¼ cup mayonnaise in a small mixing bowl; stir well. Cover and refrigerate.

Cut each slice of bread with a 2½-inch biscuit cutter. Spread half of bread rounds lightly with additional mayonnaise, and top each with 1 heaping teaspoon of chilled celery mixture.

Cut out centers of remaining bread rounds with a 1-inch biscuit cutter, and reserve for other uses. Place cut-out bread rounds on top of celery mixture to make sandwiches. Serve immediately. Yield: 1½ dozen.

Note: Celery mixture may be covered and refrigerated overnight, if desired.

CHUTNEY SANDWICHES

12 slices thin-sliced white bread, crust removed
¼ cup butter or margarine, softened
1 (9-ounce) jar chutney
1 (8-ounce) package cream cheese, softened

Cut each bread slice into 4 squares. Spread butter evenly over each square; spread ½ teaspoon chutney evenly over buttered squares.

Beat cream cheese in a small mixing bowl until light and fluffy. Spoon cream cheese into a pastry bag fitted with a star tip, and pipe around edge of each sandwich. Chill. Yield: 4 dozen.

An "at home" party is meant to be an informal occasion, with refreshments kept on the light side. It usually takes the form of a drop-in visit with prior knowledge that a hostess will be available.

Parrots, palms, and people thrive on sunny Texas days, or so it seems in this 1910 photograph of a Houston family enjoying their porch.

SAND TARTS

2 cups all-purpose flour
¼ cup plus 2 tablespoons
  sifted powdered sugar
1 cup butter
1 teaspoon ice water
½ cup chopped
  pecans
Additional sifted powdered
  sugar

Combine flour and ¼ cup plus 2 tablespoons powdered sugar in a medium mixing bowl; cut in butter with a pastry blender until mixture resembles coarse meal. Add water and pecans, stirring just until dry ingredients are moistened.

Roll dough into 1-inch balls, and place 2 inches apart on ungreased cookie sheets. Bake at 350° for 6 to 8 minutes. Cool slightly on cookie sheets; roll warm cookies in additional powdered sugar, and cool completely on wire racks. Yield: about 5 dozen.

CHOCOLATE CREAM DROPS

1 egg white
3 tablespoons water
4 cups powdered sugar
8 (1-ounce) squares
  semisweet chocolate
¾ cup finely grated paraffin

Combine egg white and water in a medium mixing bowl; beat lightly. Add powdered sugar, 1 cup at a time, stirring well after each addition.

Shape mixture into 1-inch balls; shape each ball into a cone. Place on waxed paper-lined baking sheets; let stand overnight.

Combine chocolate and paraffin in top of a double boiler. Cook over simmering water, stirring constantly, until mixture melts; remove from heat, leaving chocolate mixture in top of double boiler over hot water. Dip cone-shaped candies in melted chocolate mixture to cover completely. Place candies on waxed paper-lined baking sheets; refrigerate until chocolate coating hardens. Yield: about 5 dozen.

SPICED RUM TEA

1 cup water
3 tablespoons whole
  cloves
2 quarts unsweetened tea
1 (46-ounce) can pineapple
  juice
⅔ cup orange juice
¼ cup plus 2 tablespoons
  lemon juice
¾ cup sugar
Light rum

Bring water to a boil in a small saucepan; stir in cloves. Reduce heat, and simmer, uncovered, 3 minutes. Strain mixture, discarding cloves.

Combine boiled water, tea, pineapple juice, orange juice, lemon juice, and sugar in a large Dutch oven; stir well. Cook over medium heat until sugar dissolves and mixture is thoroughly heated.

Stir 1 tablespoon rum into each 1 cup serving. Serve hot. Yield: about 1 gallon.

MARION HARLAND'S
AFTERNOON TEA PARTY

Tea was a man's drink when first introduced into London coffee houses in the 1650s. Women clung to wine and ale until around 1662, when King Charles II's Portuguese Queen Catherine made tea popular at court. Nineteenth-century American writers wrote copiously on tea protocol. One of the most credible of them was Marion Harland, who thought of herself as a novelist first, cookbook writer second. The wife of a clergyman, she was known for her charming parties. Women knew that her 1875 *Breakfast, Luncheon and Tea* would tell them everything they needed to know for a successful tea party. The menu that follows would have met with her approval.

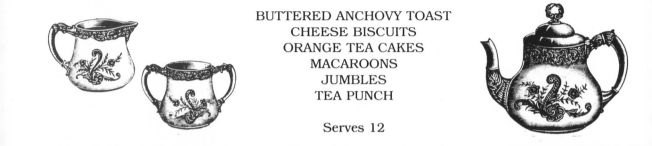

BUTTERED ANCHOVY TOAST
CHEESE BISCUITS
ORANGE TEA CAKES
MACAROONS
JUMBLES
TEA PUNCH

Serves 12

Members of the Flagler family at tea in the style of Marion Harland, 1896.

BUTTERED ANCHOVY TOAST

12 slices toast, crust removed
2 tablespoons butter or
    margarine, softened
1 (.1-ounce) tube anchovy
    paste
Fresh parsley sprigs

Cut various shapes from toast, using assorted canapé cutters; spread each toast shape evenly with butter and ¼ teaspoon anchovy paste. Transfer canapés to a serving platter, and garnish with parsley sprigs. Yield: 3 dozen.

CHEESE BISCUITS

1 cup all-purpose flour
¼ teaspoon salt
Dash of red pepper
⅓ cup shortening
2 to 3 tablespoons cold water
1½ cups (6 ounces) grated
    sharp Cheddar cheese,
    divided
1 egg, beaten

Combine flour, salt, and pepper in a medium mixing bowl; cut in shortening with a pastry blender until mixture resembles coarse meal. Sprinkle water evenly over flour mixture, stirring until dry ingredients are moistened. Shape dough into a ball; chill at least 1 hour.

Roll dough to ⅛-inch thickness on a lightly floured surface; sprinkle ½ cup cheese over surface. Roll up jellyroll fashion. Roll jellyroll-shaped dough to ⅛-inch thickness, and sprinkle with ½ cup cheese; roll up jellyroll fashion. Cover and chill.

Repeat rolling procedure with jellyroll-shaped dough. Cut into 2-inch squares or triangles, using a pastry wheel. Place on ungreased baking sheets. Bake at 400° for 10 minutes or until lightly browned. Brush biscuits with beaten egg; sprinkle remaining cheese evenly over biscuits. Continue baking 2 minutes or until cheese melts. Serve warm. Yield: about 3 dozen.

Orange Tea Cakes (front) and Jumbles for a tea.

ORANGE TEA CAKES

¼ cup butter or margarine
1½ teaspoons grated orange
    rind
½ cup sugar
1 egg
1 cup all-purpose flour
1 teaspoon baking powder
¼ teaspoon salt
¼ cup orange juice
2 tablespoons milk
Orange Butter Frosting

Cream butter and orange rind; gradually add sugar, beating well. Add egg; beat well.

Combine flour, baking powder, and salt; add to creamed mixture alternately with orange juice and milk, beginning and ending with flour mixture. Beat well after each addition.

Spoon batter into greased miniature muffin pans, filling two-thirds full. Bake at 375° for 12 to 15 minutes. Cool in pans 10 minutes; remove to wire racks to cool completely. Spread cakes evenly with Orange Butter Frosting. Yield: 2½ dozen.

Orange Butter Frosting:

2 tablespoons butter,
    softened
1 cup sifted powdered sugar
½ teaspoon grated orange
    rind
1 tablespoon orange juice
½ teaspoon vanilla extract

Cream butter and sugar. Gradually add orange rind and juice, beating until light and fluffy. Add vanilla; beat until smooth. Yield: frosting for 2½ dozen tea cakes.

MACAROONS

3 egg whites
1½ cups sifted powdered
  sugar
1 (8-ounce) can almond
  paste

Beat egg whites (at room temperature) in a medium mixing bowl until foamy. Gradually add sugar, 2 tablespoons at a time, beating until stiff peaks form.

Cream almond paste in a medium mixing bowl. Add to egg white mixture, beating well. Chill overnight.

Preheat oven to 400°. Drop chilled dough by rounded teaspoonfuls 2 inches apart onto lightly greased parchment-lined cookie sheets. Reduce heat to 300°, and bake for 10 to 12 minutes. Cool completely on cookie sheets. Carefully remove from parchment, and store in airtight containers. Yield: about 4 dozen.

JUMBLES

½ cup butter or margarine,
  softened
¾ cup sugar
2 egg yolks, beaten
1¼ cups all-purpose flour
2 tablespoons sherry
½ teaspoon vanilla extract

Cream butter in a medium mixing bowl; gradually add sugar, beating until light and fluffy. Add egg yolks; mix well. Stir in flour until well blended. Add sherry and vanilla; stir well. Cover and chill 2 to 3 hours.

Shape dough into ¾-inch balls; place 2 inches apart on lightly greased parchment-lined cookie sheets. Bake at 350° for 8 minutes or until lightly browned. Cool slightly on cookie sheets; remove from parchment, and cool completely on wire racks. Yield: about 4 dozen.

TEA PUNCH

2 quarts water
2 tablespoons plus 2
  teaspoons tea leaves
2 to 2½ cups sugar
½ cup plus 2 tablespoons
  lemon juice
Ice ring
1 quart carbonated mineral
  water
1 pint fresh strawberries,
  washed and hulled

Bring water to a boil in a large Dutch oven; pour over tea leaves in a large pitcher or mixing bowl. Cover and let steep 5 minutes; strain, discarding tea leaves. Chill thoroughly.

Combine sugar and lemon juice in a small mixing bowl, stirring well. Add to chilled tea, stirring well.

Pour tea over ice ring in a punch bowl 15 minutes before serving. Stir in carbonated water and strawberries just before serving. Yield: about 3 quarts.

The "MARION HARLAND" COFFEE POT AND PROCESS OF COFFEE MAKING

BOILING WATER

STRAINER

VALVE

GROUND COFFEE IN FILTER

COFFEE INFUSION

In the 1870s, Marion Harland lent her name to several consumer products.

Such a dressy tea would certainly have been mentioned in the press. Photograph c.1900.

VICTORIAN TEA

The term Victorian can be a somewhat contradictory adjective: fussy elegance, strait-laced opulence. But it adequately describes the elaborate teas given by society leaders throughout the South in the early 1900s. Newspaper hyperbole was at a peak: if Mrs. Dismukes wore her blue foulard to Mrs. Willoughby's tea, the press drew word pictures of it. Men gave teas, too, as when Navy Lt. J.A. Tobin entertained for W.V. Chapin at the St. Augustine Golf Club. Pretty ladies poured the beverages; tea cakes, delicate sandwiches, and confections comprised the menu.

HERBED PARTY TRIANGLES
HAM SANDWICHES * CALLA LILY SANDWICHES
CHEESE CRESCENTS
GRILLED ALMONDS
VICTORIAN TEA CAKES * PETTICOAT TAILS
PEPPERMINT DROPS * CANDIED CITRUS PEEL
FIVE O'CLOCK TEA
AFTERNOON CHOCOLATE
ROSE LEAF PUNCH

Serves 24

HERBED PARTY TRIANGLES

1 (8-ounce) package cream
  cheese, softened
1 tablespoon catsup
¾ teaspoon salt
¼ teaspoon pepper
¾ cup chopped almonds
¼ cup chopped green pepper
¼ cup chopped onion
3 tablespoons chopped
  pimiento
18 slices thin-sliced rye
  bread, crust removed

Beat cream cheese in a medium mixing bowl; add catsup, salt, and pepper, beating until smooth. Stir in almonds, green pepper, onion, and pimiento.

Spread bread slices evenly with mixture. Cut each slice into 4 triangles. Yield: 6 dozen.

HAM SANDWICHES

½ cup butter or margarine,
  softened
1 egg yolk
1 teaspoon vinegar or pickle
  juice
2 teaspoons dry mustard
¼ teaspoon red pepper
Dash of salt
2 cups cooked,
  ground ham
24 slices white bread, crust
  removed
Miniature sweet pickle slices

Combine first 6 ingredients; mix well. Stir in ground ham.

Cut each bread slice into four 1-inch diamond shapes. Spread ham mixture on half of diamond shapes; top with remaining diamond shapes. Place a pickle slice on top of each sandwich; secure with a wooden pick. Yield: 4 dozen.

CALLA LILY SANDWICHES

1 (8-ounce) package cream
  cheese, softened
2 tablespoons whipping
  cream
1 teaspoon onion juice
¼ teaspoon garlic salt
1 (1-pound) package process
  cheese spread
24 slices thin-sliced white
  bread, crust removed
Finely chopped fresh parsley

Combine cream cheese, whipping cream, onion juice, and garlic salt in a small mixing bowl; beat until light and fluffy. Set aside.

Cut cheese into ¼-inch-thick slices; cut each slice into 2- x ¼-inch strips. Gently roll each strip to form a 2-inch-long cylinder, forming the stamen. Set aside.

Cut each bread slice into a 3-inch square. Trim corners to form a teardrop shape, leaving one corner intact. Spread with reserved cream cheese mixture.

Place a reserved cheese roll across each teardrop, with one end of the roll at the untrimmed corner. Gently overlap bread at corner, and pinch to form base of lily. Spread base lightly with cream cheese mixture; sprinkle with chopped parsley. Repeat procedure with remaining bread slices and cheese rolls. Yield: 2 dozen.

CHEESE CRESCENTS

2¼ cups all-purpose flour
⅛ teaspoon salt
½ teaspoon red pepper
Dash of paprika
¾ cup butter or margarine
2 cups (8 ounces) shredded
  sharp Cheddar cheese

Sift together first 4 ingredients in a large mixing bowl; cut in butter with a pastry blender until mixture resembles coarse meal. Stir in cheese.

Turn dough out onto a floured surface, and knead lightly 3 to 4 times. Shape dough into a ball; cover at least 1 hour.

Work with one-fourth of dough at a time, keeping remaining dough chilled. Shape dough into small crescents, using 1 tablespoon dough for each crescent; place on lightly greased baking sheets, and bake at 400° for 8 minutes or until lightly browned. Cool slightly on baking sheets; remove to wire racks to cool completely. Yield: about 6 dozen.

GRILLED ALMONDS

2 cups sugar
½ cup water
2 cups blanched almonds

Combine sugar and water in a medium saucepan; cook over medium heat, stirring constantly, until sugar dissolves. Continue cooking, without stirring, until mixture reaches thread stage (230°). Add almonds; continue to cook over high heat, without stirring, until mixture reaches hard ball stage (260°). Remove from heat. Stir mixture until sugar crystallizes on almonds.

Working rapidly, separate almonds into a single layer on a buttered 15- x 10- x 1-inch jellyroll pan. Let cool. Yield: 24 servings.

Lavishly appointed drawing room is a stage for opulent clothing, dainty foods, and tea, c.1900.

VICTORIAN TEA CAKES

1 cup butter, softened
2 cups sugar
3 cups all-purpose flour
2 teaspoons baking powder
¼ teaspoon salt
1 cup ice water
1 teaspoon almond extract
6 egg whites
1 cup apricot jam
Icing (recipe follows)
Royal Icing (page 71)

Grease a 13- x 9- x 2-inch baking pan, and line with waxed paper. Lightly grease waxed paper, and set aside.

Cream butter; gradually add sugar, beating until light and fluffy. Combine flour, baking powder, and salt; add to creamed mixture alternately with ice water; mix well. Stir in almond flavoring.

Beat egg whites (at room temperature) in a large mixing bowl until soft peaks form; fold into creamed mixture. Pour batter into prepared pan. Bake at 325° for 50 minutes or until a wooden pick inserted in center comes out clean. Cool in pan 10 minutes. Remove to a wire rack; discard waxed paper, and cool completely.

Wrap cake in aluminum foil. Freeze until firm; slice horizontally, separating layers.

Heat jam over low heat, stirring frequently, until jam melts. Spread on bottom layer, and replace top layer.

Cut cake into assorted shapes, using 1¾-inch cookie cutters. Place cakes 2 inches apart on a wire rack; place rack in shallow pan. Quickly pour warm icing over cakes, covering the top and sides.

Spoon up all icing that drips through rack, and reheat to 110°; add a small amount of water, if necessary, to maintain original consistency. Continue pouring and reheating until cakes are smoothly and evenly coated. (This may take 2 to 3 coatings.) Allow icing to dry.

Place cakes on a cutting board; using a sharp knife, trim any surplus icing.

Victorian Tea Cakes with Five O'Clock Tea. The latter is laced with rum.

Tint Royal Icing, if desired; spoon into pastry bag fitted with a No. 2 or 3 round tip. Pipe simple designs on cakes, as desired. Yield: about 2½ dozen.

Icing:

7 cups sifted powdered sugar
½ cup plus 3 tablespoons water
3 tablespoons light corn syrup
1 teaspoon almond extract
Paste food coloring

Combine all ingredients in a saucepan; cook over low heat, stirring constantly, until icing reaches pouring consistency (about 110°). Use white icing before tinting remaining icing with desired colors. Yield: icing for 2½ dozen tea cakes.

PETTICOAT TAILS

5 cups all-purpose flour
1 cup sifted powdered sugar
2 cups butter

Sift together flour and sugar in a large mixing bowl; cut in butter with a pastry blender until mixture resembles coarse meal. Shape mixture into a roll, 2 inches in diameter. Wrap in waxed paper; chill 30 minutes.

Unwrap roll, and cut into ¼-inch slices. Place on ungreased cookie sheets. Press the floured tines of a fork around edge of each cookie. Bake at 350° for 8 to 10 minutes. Yield: about 9 dozen.

PEPPERMINT DROPS

2 cups sugar
¼ cup light corn syrup
¼ cup milk
¼ teaspoon cream of
 tartar
⅛ teaspoon peppermint oil
Royal Icing

Combine sugar, syrup, milk, and cream of tartar in a large saucepan, stirring well. Cook over low heat, stirring constantly, until mixture comes to a boil. Cover and continue boiling 3 minutes. (This allows the condensation from the steam to wash the sugar crystals from the sides of the pan.) Uncover and continue cooking, without stirring, until mixture reaches soft ball stage (234°). Remove from heat, and let mixture cool slightly.

Add peppermint oil, and beat with a wire whisk until mixture becomes creamy. Immediately place saucepan in hot water to keep mixture from hardening. Working rapidly, drop by teaspoonfuls onto waxed paper-lined baking sheets; cool completely. Decorate as desired with Royal Icing. Yield: about 4 dozen.

Royal Icing:

1 egg white
⅛ teaspoon cream of
 tartar
1 cup plus 3 tablespoons
 sifted powdered sugar
Paste food coloring

Combine egg white (at room temperature) and cream of tartar in a medium mixing bowl. Beat at medium speed of an electric mixer until foamy. Add powdered sugar, 2 tablespoons at a time, beating at high speed of an electric mixer 5 minutes or until stiff peaks form.

Color small amounts of icing with desired colors. Spoon icing into a pastry bag fitted with a round tip. Decorate mints with delicate bows or as desired. Yield: about ¾ cup.

Note: Icing dries very quickly; keep covered at all times with a damp cloth or plastic wrap.

CANDIED CITRUS PEEL

Rind of 3 oranges
Rind of 3 lemons
Rind of 1 medium grapefruit
1 tablespoon salt
2½ cups sugar, divided
½ cup water

Cut rind into ¼-inch-wide strips. Combine rind, salt, and water to cover in a large mixing bowl; cover and refrigerate overnight.

Drain, discarding water. Place rind in a large non-metallic saucepan with water to cover; bring to a boil. Reduce heat; simmer, uncovered, 45 minutes. Drain, discarding liquid. Repeat cooking procedure two more times.

Combine 1½ cups sugar and ½ cup water in a medium saucepan, stirring to dissolve sugar. Bring to a boil; add rind. Reduce heat; simmer, uncovered, stirring occasionally, until syrup is absorbed.

Roll strips, a few at a time, in remaining sugar. Arrange in a single layer on wire racks; let dry 5 hours. Store in an airtight container. Yield: 24 servings.

FIVE O'CLOCK TEA

1½ gallons cold water
½ cup tea leaves
24 sugar cubes
½ cup light rum, divided
Lemon slices

Bring water to a boil in a large stockpot; pour over tea leaves in another large stockpot. Cover and let steep 10 minutes. Strain, discarding tea leaves.

Pour hot tea into individual cups containing 1 sugar cube, 1 teaspoon rum, and 1 lemon slice. Serve immediately. Yield: about 1½ gallons.

AFTERNOON CHOCOLATE

6 (1-ounce) squares
 unsweetened chocolate,
 grated
1½ cups sugar
¼ teaspoon salt
1½ quarts water
1 tablespoon cornstarch
1½ quarts milk, scalded and
 divided
Whipped cream

Combine first 4 ingredients in a Dutch oven. Cook over medium heat, stirring constantly, until mixture comes to a boil. Remove from heat; cool.

Dissolve cornstarch in ¼ cup milk, stirring well; add cornstarch mixture and remaining milk to reserved chocolate mixture. Cook over low heat, stirring constantly, until mixture is thoroughly heated. Pour into cups, and serve immediately with a dollop of whipped cream. Yield: 3 quarts.

ROSE LEAF PUNCH

1½ cups water
½ cup sugar
1½ cups Curaçao or other
 orange-flavored liqueur
1 cup brandy
Ice molds
3 (25.4-ounce) bottles
 champagne, chilled
American Beauty Rose petals
 (optional)

Combine water and sugar in a small saucepan. Cook over medium heat, stirring constantly, until sugar dissolves. Remove from heat, and chill.

Pour sugar water, Curaçao, and brandy over individual ice molds in a punch bowl. Gradually add champagne just before serving. Garnish base of punch bowl with rose petals, if desired. Yield: about 1 gallon.

Note: Rose buds may be frozen in individual molds to float in punch.

GARDEN TEA AT MAGNOLIA GROVE

Ask anyone who has lived in the South to imagine the perfect setting for an informal outdoor tea. The vision: a magnolia-scented garden surrounding a columned Greek Revival house just like the one at Greensboro, Alabama. Built in 1835 by Colonel Issac Croom, Magnolia Grove is now a state shrine open to the public. Croom helped found the University of the South at Sewanee, Tennessee. Before coming under the protection of the state, Magnolia Grove was owned by the Hobson family. Total beauty under ancient magnolias is the backdrop for this summery tea.

MELON BALLS IN MINT-RUM SAUCE
SHRIMP PASTE SANDWICHES
CHICKEN SALAD IN CHEESE PUFFS
MERINGUE SHELLS WITH LEMON CURD
GLAZED ORANGE-FROSTED BROWNIES
MINT-FROSTED BROWNIES
TEA

Serves 10 to 15

MELON BALLS IN MINT-RUM SAUCE

- 2 **medium cantaloupes, halved and seeded**
- 2 **medium honeydew melons, halved and seeded**
- 2 **cups water**
- ½ **cup sugar**
- 3 **cups fresh mint leaves**
- ¼ **cup light rum**
- ¼ **cup melon liqueur**

Scoop out melon balls; place in a large mixing bowl. Cover and refrigerate.

Combine water, sugar, and mint in a medium saucepan; bring to a boil. Reduce heat; simmer, uncovered, 10 minutes. Strain, discarding mint; chill thoroughly. Add rum and melon liqueur, stirring well.

Pour sauce over reserved melon balls, stirring gently. Cover and refrigerate overnight. Yield: 10 to 15 servings.

SHRIMP PASTE SANDWICHES

- ½ **pound cooked shrimp, peeled and deveined**
- ¼ **cup butter, softened**
- 1 **tablespoon lemon juice**
- 2 **teaspoons sherry**
- ½ **teaspoon dry mustard**
- ⅛ **teaspoon salt**
- **Dash of mace**
- 12 **slices thin-sliced white bread, crust removed**
- **Fresh parsley sprigs**

Process shrimp in an electric blender until coarsely ground. Combine ground shrimp and butter; stir well. Add lemon juice, sherry, mustard, salt, and mace; mix well. Chill.

Roll bread slices flat with a rolling pin. Spread shrimp paste on each bread slice, and roll up jellyroll fashion. Chill.

Cut rolls into 3 equal portions. Tuck a sprig of parsley into one end of each rolled section. Yield: 3 dozen.

Magnolia Grove, a classic Southern setting, c.1904.

Alabama Historical Commission

Melon Balls in Mint-Rum Sauce with Chicken Salad in Cheese Puffs, Glazed Orange- and Mint-Frosted Brownies, and Meringue Shells with Lemon Curd.

Richmond Pearson Hobson, third gentleman from left, at Magnolia Grove, 1894.

CHICKEN SALAD IN CHEESE PUFFS

2 cups finely chopped, cooked chicken
¼ cup finely chopped celery
¼ cup sliced almonds
2 tablespoons finely chopped green onion
2 tablespoons finely chopped pimiento
2 tablespoons white wine
½ teaspoon salt
¼ teaspoon lemon juice
Dash of pepper
½ cup mayonnaise
Cheese Puffs

Combine all ingredients, except mayonnaise and Cheese Puffs, in a medium mixing bowl; toss lightly. Stir in mayonnaise; chill thoroughly.

Cut tops off Cheese Puffs, and fill each with 1 heaping teaspoon salad. Replace tops, and serve immediately. Yield: about 3 dozen.

Cheese Puffs:

¼ cup butter or margarine
½ cup water
½ cup all-purpose flour
⅛ teaspoon salt
2 eggs, beaten
½ cup (2 ounces) shredded Swiss cheese

Combine butter and water in a heavy saucepan; bring to a boil over medium heat, stirring until butter melts. Add flour and salt, stirring vigorously until mixture leaves sides of pan and forms a smooth ball. Remove from heat, and cool slightly. Add eggs, stirring until well blended. Return to heat, and beat until smooth. Stir in cheese.

Drop batter by heaping teaspoonfuls onto greased baking sheets. Bake at 400° for 15 minutes or until puffed and golden brown. Remove puffs to wire racks, and cool completely. Yield: about 3 dozen.

MERINGUE SHELLS WITH LEMON CURD

4 egg whites
⅛ teaspoon cream of tartar
1 teaspoon vanilla
1 cup sugar
Lemon Curd
Fresh mint sprigs (optional)

Beat egg whites (at room temperature), cream of tartar, and vanilla in a large mixing bowl until foamy. Gradually add sugar, 1 tablespoon at a time, beating until stiff peaks form and sugar dissolves. (Do not under beat mixture.) Spoon meringue mixture into a pastry bag fitted with a star tip.

Draw 24 circles, 2 inches in diameter, on 2 parchment-lined baking sheets. Starting at center of each outlined circle, pipe meringue in a flat spiral fashion, using a circular motion that ends just inside each circle's outline. (This forms base of meringue cup.) Continue to pipe meringue atop outer ring of base, using a circular motion, to form 2 continuously attached and stacked meringue rings.

(These form sides of meringue cup.) Repeat procedure with remaining meringue mixture.

Bake at 225° for 1 hour. Turn oven off; cool meringues in oven at least 1 hour. (Do not open oven door.) Remove baked meringue cups from parchment. Use immediately or store in airtight containers.

Spoon Lemon Curd evenly into each cup. Garnish with mint sprigs, if desired. Yield: 2 dozen.

Lemon Curd:

3 eggs, beaten
⅔ cup sugar
⅓ cup fresh lemon juice
2 tablespoons butter or margarine, softened

Combine eggs, sugar, lemon juice, and butter in a non-aluminum saucepan. Cook over medium-low heat, stirring constantly, until thickened and bubbly. Let cool. Chill thoroughly before spooning into shells. Yield: about 2 cups.

GLAZED ORANGE-FROSTED BROWNIES

¾ cup all-purpose flour
¼ teaspoon baking soda
¼ teaspoon salt
½ cup sugar
⅓ cup shortening
2 tablespoons water
1 (6-ounce) package
    semisweet chocolate
    morsels
1 teaspoon vanilla extract
2 eggs
1½ cups coarsely chopped
    walnuts
¼ cup dark rum
Orange Frosting
Chocolate Glaze

Sift together flour, soda, and salt in a medium mixing bowl; set aside.

Combine sugar, shortening, and water in a medium saucepan; cook over medium heat, stirring constantly, until mixture comes to a boil. Remove from heat; add chocolate morsels and vanilla, stirring until chocolate melts. Add eggs, one at a time, beating with a wire whisk after each addition. Stir in reserved flour mixture and walnuts, mixing well.

Pour batter evenly into a greased 9-inch square baking pan. Bake at 325° for 25 minutes or until a wooden pick inserted in center comes out clean. Sprinkle rum evenly over brownies; cool completely.

Spread Orange Frosting evenly over cooled brownies; chill until set.

Spread Chocolate Glaze evenly over frosted brownies; chill until set.

Allow brownies to come to room temperature before cutting into 1½-inch squares. Yield: 3 dozen.

Orange Frosting:

⅓ cup butter or margarine,
    softened
1 teaspoon grated orange rind
2 cups sifted powdered sugar
2 tablespoons orange juice
Orange paste food coloring

Cream butter and orange rind in a medium mixing bowl. Add sugar alternately with orange juice, beating well. Add a small amount of food coloring, mixing well. Yield: frosting for one 9-inch square cake.

Chocolate Glaze:

1 (6-ounce) package
    semisweet chocolate
    morsels
1 tablespoon shortening

Combine chocolate morsels and shortening in top of a double boiler; cook over simmering water, stirring constantly, until mixture melts. Remove from heat, and cool to room temperature. Yield: glaze for one 9-inch square cake.

MINT-FROSTED BROWNIES

½ cup butter or margarine,
    softened
½ cup sugar
2 eggs
2 (1-ounce) squares
    semisweet chocolate,
    melted
½ cup all-purpose flour
1 teaspoon vanilla extract
½ cup chopped pecans
Mint Frosting
Chocolate Glaze

Cream butter in a medium mixing bowl; gradually add sugar, beating well. Add eggs, beating well. Add melted chocolate; beat well. Gradually stir in flour and vanilla. Fold in pecans.

Pour batter into a greased 8-inch square baking pan. Bake at 350° for 20 to 25 minutes. Cool completely in pan.

Spread Mint Frosting evenly over cooled brownies. Let stand until set.

Pour Chocolate Glaze over frosted brownies. Spread evenly over entire surface. Chill at least 1 hour. Cut into 2-inch squares. Yield: about 1½ dozen.

Mint Frosting:

2 tablespoons butter or
    margarine, softened
1 cup sifted powdered sugar
1 tablespoon milk
½ teaspoon peppermint
    extract
1 drop green food coloring

Combine all ingredients in a medium mixing bowl; beat until mixture is smooth. Yield: frosting for one 8-inch square cake.

Chocolate Glaze:

2 (1-ounce) squares
    semisweet chocolate
2 tablespoons butter or
    margarine

Combine chocolate and butter in top of a double boiler; place over simmering water, stirring constantly, until mixture melts. Remove from heat, and cool to room temperature. Yield: glaze for one 8-inch square cake.

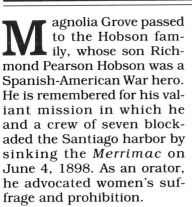

Magnolia Grove passed to the Hobson family, whose son Richmond Pearson Hobson was a Spanish-American War hero. He is remembered for his valiant mission in which he and a crew of seven blockaded the Santiago harbor by sinking the *Merrimac* on June 4, 1898. As an orator, he advocated women's suffrage and prohibition.

New York Public Library

Judge Robert A. Hefner's home, which was given to Oklahoma City. Photograph c.1940.

ART LEAGUE TEA AT THE HEFNER HOME

How often we read of a historic mansion saved from the wrecking ball and restored at enormous expense. Not so with The Heritage House in Oklahoma City. The mansion, complete with priceless antique collections, was an outright gift to his beloved state from a favorite son, Robert A. Hefner. The Hefner family occupied the home from 1927 to 1970, during which time Hefner had retired as Justice of the State Supreme Court, traveled the world with his wife, collecting treasures for their home, and served two terms as Mayor. Judge and Mrs. Hefner hosted the Oklahoma Art League's Registration Tea at their home in 1945.

CRAB SALAD SANDWICHES
CARROT SANDWICHES
FOUR O'CLOCK TEA SCONES
PASTEL CREAM WAFERS
CHERRY TARTS
MOCHA MILK PUNCH
HOT TEA

Serves 15 to 20

CRABMEAT SANDWICHES

1 pound lump or flake
   crabmeat, drained
1 cup chopped celery
½ cup mayonnaise
16 slices white bread,
   toasted and crust
   removed
Paprika

Combine crabmeat, celery, and mayonnaise in a medium mixing bowl; mix well.

Spread crab mixture evenly over all slices of bread. Cut each sandwich into 2 triangles; sprinkle with paprika. Yield: about 2½ dozen.

CARROT SANDWICHES

2 cups grated carrot
¼ cup chopped ripe olives
2 tablespoons minced onion
½ cup mayonnaise
48 slices whole wheat bread,
   crust removed
Additional mayonnaise
Sliced ripe olives

Combine carrot, chopped olives, onion, and ½ cup mayonnaise in a medium mixing bowl; stir well.

Cut 2 rounds from each slice of bread with a fluted 2-inch round cutter. Spread a small amount of additional mayonnaise and carrot mixture evenly over half of bread rounds; cut out center of each remaining round with a ½-inch round cutter (reserve for other uses); place fluted rounds over carrot mixture to make sandwiches. Garnish each sandwich with olive slices. Serve immediately. Yield: 4 dozen.

Note: Carrot mixture may be covered and refrigerated overnight, if desired.

Teapots are collectibles. This nineteenth-century die-cut of a teapot with harbor scene would be a prize in anyone's collection.

FOUR O'CLOCK TEA SCONES

4 cups all-purpose
   flour
¼ cup sugar
2 tablespoons baking
   powder
2 teaspoons salt
¼ cup plus 2 tablespoons
   butter or margarine
1 cup milk
2 eggs, lightly beaten
Additional butter or
   margarine, melted
Additional sugar

Sift together flour, ¼ cup sugar, baking powder, and salt in a medium mixing bowl; cut ¼ cup plus 2 tablespoons butter into flour mixture with a pastry blender until mixture resembles coarse meal. Gradually add milk and beaten eggs; stir with a fork just until dry ingredients are moistened.

Turn dough out onto a floured surface, and knead 4 to 5 times. Roll dough to ¼-inch thickness; cut with a 1½-inch biscuit cutter. Place scones on greased baking sheets; brush with melted butter, and sprinkle evenly with additional sugar. Bake at 400° for 12 minutes or until lightly browned. Yield: about 3 dozen.

PASTEL CREAM WAFERS

1¼ cups butter, softened and
   divided
2 cups all-purpose flour
⅓ cup whipping cream
¼ cup sugar
¾ cup sifted powdered sugar
1 egg yolk
1 teaspoon almond extract
Liquid food coloring (optional)

Combine 1 cup butter, flour, and whipping cream in a medium mixing bowl, mixing well; cover and chill thoroughly.

Roll dough to ⅛-inch thickness on a lightly floured surface; cut with a 1½-inch biscuit cutter. Gently press each round into ¼ cup sugar in a small mixing bowl, turning to coat both sides. Place on ungreased cookie sheets, and prick each round several times with a wooden pick. Bake at 375° for 5 minutes. Remove from cookie sheets, and cool on wire racks.

Combine remaining butter, powdered sugar, egg yolk, and almond extract in a small mixing bowl, beating well. Tint with food coloring, if desired.

Spread a small amount of filling over half of wafers; top with remaining wafers. Yield: about 4 dozen.

Mocha Milk Punch tastes as delightful as camellias look.

CHERRY TARTS

1 (16-ounce) can red tart
   cherries, undrained
1 cup sugar
2 tablespoons cornstarch
1 teaspoon lemon juice
Pâte Brisée Sucrée
Whipped cream

Drain cherries, reserving liquid. Set aside.

Combine sugar and cornstarch in a medium saucepan. Gradually stir in reserved cherry juice and lemon juice. Cook over medium heat, stirring constantly, 10 minutes or until thickened and bubbly. Stir in cherries. Remove from heat, and cool. Spoon 2 teaspoons cherry filling into each Pâte Brisée Sucrée tart shell. Garnish each tart with a dollop of whipped cream. Yield: eighteen 1¾-inch tarts.

Pâte Brisée Sucrée:

1½ cups all-purpose
   flour
2 tablespoons sugar
½ teaspoon salt
½ cup butter, chilled
1 egg yolk
¼ cup half-and-half

Combine flour, sugar, and salt; cut in butter with a pastry blender until mixture resembles coarse meal. Combine egg yolk and half-and-half; add to flour mixture. Stir with a fork until dry ingredients are moistened. Shape dough into a ball; chill thoroughly.

Roll dough to ⅛-inch thickness on a lightly floured surface; cut into rounds with a fluted 2-inch round cutter. Fit each pastry into a 1¾-inch muffin pan; prick pastry shells with a fork. Bake at 400° for 10 to 12 minutes. Yield: 1½ dozen.

MOCHA MILK PUNCH

1 quart coffee ice cream,
   divided
2 cups strong coffee, chilled
   and divided
2 cups milk, divided
½ cup bourbon, divided
½ cup light rum, divided
½ cup crème de cacao,
   divided
Additional coffee ice cream
Sifted cocoa (optional)

Combine half of all ingredients, except additional ice cream, in container of an electric blender; process until smooth. Repeat procedure with remaining ingredients, except additional ice cream.

Pour punch into chilled bowl, and top with scoops of additional coffee ice cream. Sprinkle with sifted cocoa, if desired. Yield: about 3 quarts.

DEBUTANTE SOCIAL

In 1818, when Ann Matilda Page of Retreat Plantation, St. Simon's Island, was introduced to Savannah society, it was among the first coming out parties which became traditions in many families. Each debutante has her season of nonstop parties, enough to fill a lifetime of remembrances. Fashions must be versatile; today's deb might be found dressed in a swimsuit at a poolside social or dressed in mauve for a glamorous tea, as her grandmother was in her day. Music? "Stardust" may be out, but today's sounds may still be soft and sweet. As for the food, we can only think of it as Southern: Chicken Salad Pastries, Cucumber Sandwiches. . . .

CHICKEN SALAD IN TART SHELLS
SHRIMP AND CREAM CHEESE TRIANGLES
OPEN-FACE DATE-NUT SANDWICHES
CUCUMBER SANDWICHES
PINEAPPLE-LEMON SHERBET
COMING-OUT CAKES
GINER ALE PUNCH

Serves 20

A debutante party at the Quarry Club in Rothesay, Virginia, 1951.

CHICKEN SALAD IN TART SHELLS

1 (5- to 6-pound) baking hen
9 stalks celery, cleaned and divided
1 tablespoon salt, divided
½ teaspoon pepper
3 quarts water
8 hard-cooked eggs, chopped
1 cup mayonnaise
1 tablespoon lemon juice
½ teaspoon red pepper
½ teaspoon paprika
Tart shells (recipe follows)

Rinse hen with cold water, and place in a large stockpot. Add 1 stalk celery, 2 teaspoons salt, ½ teaspoon pepper, and water. Bring to a boil over high heat. Reduce heat; cover and simmer 2 hours, turning hen once after 1 hour. Remove from heat, and set aside to cool. Strain stock into a mixing bowl, discarding celery. Cover stock, and refrigerate. Cover hen, and refrigerate overnight.

Bone chicken, and chop meat into bite-size pieces; discard bones. Dice remaining celery. Set aside.

Carefully lift off and discard solidified fat from top of stock. Combine ½ cup broth (reserve remaining broth for other uses), reserved chicken, chopped celery, egg, mayonnaise, lemon juice, remaining salt, red pepper, and paprika in a large mixing bowl. Toss gently to mix well; chill thoroughly.

Spoon 2 tablespoons chicken salad into each tart shell. Yield: about 8 dozen.

Tart Shells:

3 cups all-purpose flour
1½ teaspoons salt
1 cup shortening
5 to 6 tablespoons ice water

Combine flour and salt in a large mixing bowl; cut in shortening with a pastry blender until mixture resembles coarse meal. Sprinkle water evenly over surface of flour mixture; stir with a fork until dry ingredients are moistened. Shape dough into a ball; chill.

Roll dough to ⅛-inch thickness on a lightly floured surface; cut into rounds with a 3½-inch cutter. Fit each pastry into a 2¾-inch tart pan; prick each with a fork. Bake at 400° for 12 to 15 minutes. Yield: about 4 dozen tart shells.

Chicken Salad in Tart Shells; Shrimp and Cream Cheese Triangles.

SHRIMP AND CREAM CHEESE TRIANGLES

½ cup mayonnaise
1 (3-ounce) package cream cheese, softened
½ teaspoon onion juice, divided
¼ teaspoon salt, divided
⅛ teaspoon dry mustard
⅛ teaspoon ground mace
6 drops hot sauce, divided
¾ pound medium shrimp, cooked, peeled, deveined, and coarsely ground
2 tablespoons minced celery
2 drops red food coloring
1 (8-ounce) package cream cheese, softened
¼ cup whipping cream
⅛ teaspoon Worcestershire sauce
2 drops green food coloring
48 slices thin-sliced white bread

Combine mayonnaise, 3 ounces cream cheese, ¼ teaspoon onion juice, ⅛ teaspoon salt, mustard, mace, and 2 drops hot sauce in a medium mixing bowl; beat until well blended. Stir in ground shrimp, celery, and red food coloring. Set aside.

Combine 8 ounces cream cheese, whipping cream, remaining onion juice, Worcestershire sauce, remaining salt, hot sauce, and green food coloring in a small mixing bowl; beat until well blended. Set aside.

Spread shrimp mixture on 16 bread slices; top each with a slice of bread. Spread cream cheese mixture evenly over tops of sandwiches. Top each with remaining bread slices. Wrap sandwiches in plastic wrap, and chill at least 1 hour. Trim crust from each sandwich. Cut each sandwich diagonally into 4 triangles. Serve immediately. Yield: about 5½ dozen.

OPEN-FACE DATE-NUT SANDWICHES

2 (3-ounce) packages cream cheese, softened
¼ cup half-and-half
1 (8-ounce) package chopped dates
½ cup chopped pecans
21 slices thin-sliced whole wheat bread, crust removed

Beat cream cheese in a medium mixing bowl; gradually add half-and-half, beating until smooth. Stir in dates and pecans.

Cut two 1¾-inch rounds or fluted rounds from each bread slice. Spread date mixture evenly on bread rounds. Yield: 3½ dozen.

CUCUMBER SANDWICHES

1 small cucumber, scored lengthwise and cut into ⅛-inch-thick slices
¼ cup vinegar
½ teaspoon salt
2 tablespoons butter or margarine, softened
2 ounces blue cheese, crumbled
2 teaspoons lemon juice
Dash of red pepper
8 slices white bread, crust removed
Paprika

Place cucumber slices with water to cover in a medium mixing bowl. Stir in vinegar and salt. Refrigerate at least 1 hour. Drain; pat cucumbers dry.

Combine butter, blue cheese, lemon juice, and pepper in a small mixing bowl; mix well.

Cut each bread slice into three 1½-inch rounds. Spread cheese mixture on each round, and top with a cucumber slice. Sprinkle paprika over each sandwich. Yield: 2 dozen.

Mary and Florence Bryan, radiant at their debut in Atlanta, 1933.

PINEAPPLE-LEMON SHERBET

5 medium lemons, cut into halves
2 cups sugar
2 cups water
2 cups pineapple juice
1 quart whipping cream
Grated lemon rind

Combine lemons, sugar, and water in a non-aluminum saucepan; bring to a boil. Reduce heat; simmer, uncovered, 20 minutes. Drain, reserving liquid; squeeze juice from lemons into reserved liquid. Stir in pineapple juice; chill.

Add whipping cream to chilled mixture, stirring well; pour mixture into a freezer can of a 1-gallon hand-turned or electric freezer. Freeze according to manufacturer's instructions. Let ripen at least 1 hour before serving. Scoop into sherbet dishes, and garnish with grated lemon rind. Serve immediately. Yield: about 1 gallon.

COMING-OUT CAKES

¾ cup butter or margarine, softened
2 cups sugar
4 eggs, separated
2½ cups all-purpose flour
2 teaspoons baking powder
½ teaspoon salt
1 cup milk
1 teaspoon vanilla extract
Pastel Icing
Royal Icing (page 71)

Cream butter in a large mixing bowl; gradually add sugar, beating well. Add egg yolks, one at a time, beating well after each addition.

Sift together flour, baking powder, and salt in a medium mixing bowl; gradually add to creamed mixture alternately with milk, beginning and ending with flour mixture. Stir in vanilla.

Beat egg whites (at room temperature) until stiff peaks form. Gently fold into batter.

Pour batter into a greased and floured 15- x 10- x 1-inch jellyroll pan. Bake at 325° for 30 minutes or until a wooden pick inserted in center comes out clean. Cool completely in pan.

Spread Pastel Icing evenly over top of cake, and allow to set slightly before marking cake off into 2½-inch squares. Decorate each square as desired with Royal Icing (page 71). Cut cake into squares, and arrange on a serving platter. Yield: 2 dozen.

Pastel Icing:

2 tablespoons butter, softened
3 cups sifted powdered sugar
¼ cup milk
¼ teaspoon salt
¾ teaspoon vanilla extract
2 drops green food coloring

Cream butter in a medium mixing bowl; add remaining ingredients, and beat until smooth. Use immediately. Yield: icing for one 15- x 10-inch cake.

GINGER ALE PUNCH

1 quart boiling water
1 tablespoon tea leaves
2½ cups sugar
1½ dozen lemons
1 dozen oranges
1 gallon orange, lime, or pineapple sherbet
2 (33.8-ounce) bottles ginger ale, chilled

Pour boiling water over tea in a large bowl; stir in sugar. Cover and steep 5 minutes. Strain, discarding tea leaves, and chill.

Squeeze juice from lemons and oranges. Strain, discarding pulp and seeds. Stir fruit juice into tea. Pour tea mixture into a large punch bowl. Scoop sherbet into punch. Add chilled ginger ale just before serving. Yield: about 1 gallon.

Early ginger ale labels from Louisiana, Florida, and South Carolina. Private collectors now avidly seek out old labels.

Houston bridal shower with Kewpie doll centerpiece, c.1925.

MOON AND SPOON BRIDAL SHOWER

I n the "Roaring Twenties," when fun and extravagance often went hand in hand, a favorite party for the bride-to-be was a "Moon and Spoon Shower." An elaborate set was constructed: a cardboard sky with stars and a back-lighted moon of silver paper. Sterling spoons in the selected pattern were fastened to the backdrop to represent, for example, the Big Dipper (six soup spoons), Venus (sugar shell), and the North Star (six iced-teas). A berry spoon "of dignity and charm" was elected the Wishing Star. The Milky Way, once the stellar attractions were in place, was a catchall for the remaining gift spoons. Cheer up; we can still manage the food!

ORANGE ICE WITH MINTED PINEAPPLE
CHICKEN WITH SOUR CREAM
STEAMED ASPARAGUS WITH HOLLANDAISE SAUCE
HEARTS OF CELERY
MINIATURE BISCUITS
CURRANT JELLY
APRICOT-MACAROON TAPIOCA
ANGEL FOOD BRIDAL CAKE
COFFEE

Serves 6

ORANGE ICE WITH MINTED PINEAPPLE

½ cup sugar
½ cup water
1 cup orange juice
1½ tablespoons lemon juice
Grated rind of 1 small orange
Minted Pineapple
6 sprigs fresh mint

Combine sugar and water in a medium saucepan; stir until well blended. Bring to a boil; boil 5 minutes, stirring occasionally. Remove from heat; stir in fruit juice and grated rind.

Pour mixture into a small stainless steel bowl; cover and freeze 4 hours or until partially frozen. Remove from freezer, and beat with an electric mixer until smooth. Cover and freeze overnight.

Place a small scoop of ice in each of 6 compotes. Spoon Minted Pineapple over each serving, and garnish with fresh mint sprigs. Serve immediately. Yield: 6 servings.

Minted Pineapple:

1 medium-size fresh
  pineapple
⅓ cup fresh mint leaves,
  crushed

Cut pineapple in half from the bottom through the crown. Remove the meat from the skin, using a curved knife. Cut pineapple into cubes. Combine pineapple cubes and crushed mint in a medium mixing bowl; mix well. Cover and refrigerate at least 8 hours.

Remove and discard crushed mint from pineapple before serving. Yield: 13 cups.

CHICKEN WITH SOUR CREAM

1 (8-ounce) carton
  commercial sour cream
1 tablespoon lemon juice
1 tablespoon Worcestershire
  sauce
1 teaspoon paprika
1 teaspoon celery salt
½ teaspoon salt
1 small clove garlic, crushed
6 chicken breast halves,
  skinned and boned
2 cups cracker crumbs
3 tablespoons butter or
  margarine, melted

Combine first 7 ingredients; mix well. Let stand 1 hour.

Dip chicken pieces in sour cream mixture; dredge in cracker crumbs. Place chicken in a single layer in an aluminum foil-lined shallow baking pan. Drizzle butter evenly over chicken. Bake, uncovered, at 350° for 35 minutes or until browned and tender. Serve immediately. Yield: 6 servings.

STEAMED ASPARAGUS WITH HOLLANDAISE SAUCE

1 cup whipping
  cream
1 egg, lightly beaten
Juice of 2 lemons
1½ teaspoons all-purpose
  flour
1 tablespoon cold
  water
½ teaspoon salt
1 tablespoon butter or
  margarine
1½ pounds fresh asparagus
  spears
Lemon twists

Combine whipping cream, egg, and lemon juice in top of a double boiler. Combine flour, water, and salt in a small bowl; stir well to make a paste. Add to whipping cream mixture. Cook over simmering water, beating constantly with a wire whisk, until mixture thickens. Remove from heat, and add butter. Continue to beat with wire whisk until butter melts. Transfer sauce to a serving container, and keep warm.

Wash asparagus spears carefully under running water to flush out sand from tips. Find the point at the end of each stalk where it breaks easily, and snap off. Line up tips, and cut off ends even with broken stalk. Remove scales with a vegetable peeler; discard stalks.

Tie asparagus into a bundle with string. Stand bundle, tips up, in bottom of double boiler. Add boiling water to fill pan half full. Cover with top of double boiler, turned upside down, for a lid. Simmer 12 minutes or until crisp-tender. Drain well.

Transfer asparagus spears to a serving platter, and snip string. Pour Hollandaise Sauce over top, and garnish platter with lemon twists. Serve immediately. Yield: 6 servings.

Note: Serve extra Hollandaise Sauce with meal.

MINIATURE BISCUITS

1 cup all-purpose flour
1½ teaspoons baking powder
½ teaspoon sugar
¼ teaspoon salt
3 tablespoons shortening
⅓ cup milk
Additional milk
Currant jelly (optional)

Combine flour, baking powder, sugar, and salt in a medium mixing bowl; stir well. Cut in shortening with a pastry blender until mixture resembles coarse meal. Add ⅓ cup milk, stirring until dry ingredients are moistened.

Turn dough out onto a floured surface; knead 4 to 5 times. Roll to ½-inch thickness; cut with a 1½-inch heart-shaped cookie cutter. Place biscuits on a lightly greased baking sheet; brush with additional milk. Bake at 450° for 8 to 10 minutes or until lightly browned. Serve with currant jelly, if desired. Yield: 1 dozen.

An Angel Food Cake becomes a bridal cake with a few well-chosen decorations: dolls, ribbons, flowers. . . .

ANGEL FOOD BRIDAL CAKE

12 egg whites
1 teaspoon cream of tartar
1 cup sugar
1 cup sifted cake flour
1 cup sifted powdered sugar
1½ teaspoons almond extract
Seven-Minute Frosting

Beat egg whites (at room temperature) until foamy. Add cream of tartar; beat until soft peaks form. Add 1 cup sugar, 2 tablespoons at a time, beating until stiff peaks form.

Sift flour and powdered sugar in a medium mixing bowl. Sprinkle flour mixture over egg white mixture, ¼ cup at a time; fold in carefully. Fold in almond extract.

Pour batter into an ungreased 10-inch tube pan; spread evenly with a spatula. Bake at 325° for 45 minutes or until cake springs back when lightly touched. Remove from oven, and invert pan. Cool 40 minutes; remove cake from pan. Frost with Seven-Minute Frosting. Yield: one 10-inch cake.

Seven-Minute Frosting:

1½ cups sugar
2 egg whites
1 tablespoon light corn syrup
Dash of salt
⅓ cup cold water
1 teaspoon vanilla extract

Combine sugar, egg whites (at room temperature), syrup, and salt in top of a large double boiler; add cold water, and beat at low speed of an electric mixer 30 seconds.

Place over boiling water; beat at high speed of an electric mixer 7 minutes or until stiff peaks form. Remove from heat. Add vanilla; beat 2 additional minutes or until frosting is thick enough to spread. Yield: frosting for one 10-inch cake.

APRICOT-MACAROON TAPIOCA

1 (17-ounce) can apricot halves, undrained
8 almond macaroons, crushed
2 cups milk, scalded
3 tablespoons instant tapioca
⅛ teaspoon salt
2 tablespoons sugar
1 egg, lightly beaten
¼ teaspoon almond extract
½ cup whipping cream, whipped
Additional whipped cream

Drain apricots, reserving juice; cut one apricot half into 6 slices, and coarsely chop remaining apricots. Cover apricots, and set aside.

Combine reserved apricot juice and macaroon crumbs in a small mixing bowl. Set aside.

Combine scalded milk, tapioca, and salt in top of a double boiler; mix well. Cook over boiling water, stirring often, 15 minutes or until mixture thickens. Stir in sugar.

Gradually stir 1 tablespoon hot tapioca mixture into beaten egg; add to remaining hot mixture, stirring well. Cook over boiling water, stirring constantly with a wire whisk, until mixture thickens.

Remove from heat; cool to room temperature. Stir in almond extract, and fold in ½ cup whipped cream. Add reserved macaroon mixture, stirring until well blended.

Spoon ¼ cup tapioca into each of 6 custard cups. Divide reserved chopped apricots equally among cups. Spoon remaining tapioca evenly over apricots. Top with additional whipped cream, and garnish each with a reserved apricot slice. Yield: 6 servings.

AFTERNOON WEDDING COLLATION

A collation is a light refreshment taken at an unusual hour as part of a celebration, like a wedding collation. Light, but oh! the magnitude of it. In 1806, Virginian William Wirt wrote of a wedding cake so large that it supported on top a 4-foot tree, which was connected to dainty foods at the table's ends by intricate paper chains. The spectacular cake was surrounded by cakes for eating and all other appropriate viands. Diaries and newspapers had different viewponts: The press of the 1800s printed reams on the decor and costumery, but of the food: "An artistic collation was served." Here is a wedding collation, Southern-style.

SHRIMP ASPIC
SESAME CHICKEN WINGS
COUNTRY PÂTÉ
RIBBON SANDWICHES
VEGETABLES WITH BLUE CHEESE WHIP
SHERRIED PECANS
WEDDING PUNCH
SPIRITED GROOM'S CAKE

Serves 48

Reception for the Martin-Connally wedding party, Atlanta, 1905.

SHRIMP ASPIC

1½ cups chili sauce
¾ cup catsup
2 envelopes unflavored
  gelatin
1 tablespoon grated onion
1 teaspoon sugar
1 teaspoon Worcestershire
  sauce
1 teaspoon prepared
  horseradish
3 tablespoons lemon juice
4 drops hot sauce
1½ pounds medium shrimp,
  cooked, peeled, deveined,
  and coarsely chopped
Fresh parsley sprigs

Combine first 9 ingredients in top of a double boiler, stirring well. Cook over simmering water, stirring constantly, until gelatin dissolves. Remove from heat. Chill until consistency of unbeaten egg white. Fold in chopped shrimp; spoon mixture into a lightly oiled 4-cup mold. Chill until firm.

Unmold aspic onto a serving platter; garnish with parsley sprigs, and serve with crackers. Yield: 16 servings.

Note: Triple recipe to serve 48 and place in two 6-cup molds.

SESAME CHICKEN WINGS

5 cups fine, dry breadcrumbs
2⅔ cups sesame seeds,
  toasted
1 tablespoon plus 1 teaspoon
  salt
1 tablespoon plus 1 teaspoon
  paprika
2 teaspoons pepper
8 dozen chicken wings
1 quart half-and-half
1½ cups butter or margarine,
  melted

Combine first 5 ingredients in a large mixing bowl; mix well. Dip chicken in half-and-half; dredge in crumb mixture.

Arrange coated wings in three 15- x 10- x 1-inch jellyroll pans. Pour melted butter evenly over chicken. Bake at 350° for 45 minutes or until golden brown. Yield: 8 dozen.

Shrimp Aspic, Country Pâté, Vegetables with Blue Cheese Whip.

COUNTRY PÂTÉ

½ pound pork fat, cut into
  strips
½ pound lean, ground pork
½ pound ground veal
½ pound ground ham
½ pound pork fat, ground
½ pound chicken livers,
  ground
2 eggs, beaten
¼ cup brandy
2 tablespoons whipping
  cream
4 cloves garlic, pressed
¼ cup all-purpose flour
2 teaspoons salt
1 teaspoon white pepper
¼ teaspoon ground allspice
¼ teaspoon ground
  cinnamon
1 bay leaf
Leaf lettuce
Green onion fan (optional)
Zucchini slices (optional)
Carrot slices (optional)
Pitted ripe olive slices
  (optional)
Watercress (optional)

Pound strips of pork fat, using a meat mallet. Line sides and bottom of a 1½-quart loafpan with flattened strips. Trim and discard excess pork fat. Set prepared loafpan aside.

Combine ground pork, veal, ham, pork fat, and chicken livers; mix well. Combine remaining ingredients, except bay leaf, lettuce, and optional ingredients; stir well. Add to ground meat mixture; mix well.

Grind entire mixture into a large mixing bowl using coarse blade of a meat grinder. Firmly press ground mixture into prepared loafpan. Place bay leaf on top. Cover with aluminum foil, and secure with string. Place loafpan in a larger shallow pan, and pour water into larger pan to a depth of 1 inch. Bake at 375° for 1½ hours.

Remove loafpan from larger pan, and cool completely. Refrigerate overnight.

Remove and discard string, aluminum foil, and bay leaf. Loosen pâté from edge of loafpan, using a sharp knife. Invert onto a lettuce-lined serving platter, and gently remove and discard fat. Place green onion fan on top of pâté, and arrange remaining optional ingredients to resemble flowers around green onion, if desired. Garnish with watercress, if desired.

Slice pâté, and serve chilled with assorted crackers. Yield: 48 appetizer servings.

A scene from a nickelodeon song slide: slides were projected as the piano player sang, c.1910.

SHERRIED PECANS

1 cup butter or margarine
2 (16-ounce) packages light
 brown sugar
1 cup sherry
2 pounds pecan halves

Melt butter in a large Dutch oven over medium heat. Add sugar and sherry. Cook over medium heat, stirring often, until mixture comes to a boil. Continue cooking, without stirring, until mixture reaches soft ball stage (240°). Remove from heat; stir in pecans.

Spread pecans on waxed paper, and separate with a spoon; cool. Yield: 48 servings.

RIBBON SANDWICHES

2 (3-ounce) packages cream
 cheese, softened
¼ cup plus 2 tablespoons
 whipping cream
2 tablespoons grated onion
2 pimientos, chopped
1 (8-ounce) package
 processed cheese spread,
 softened
¼ cup chopped
 pimiento-stuffed olives
10 slices thin-slice white
 bread, crust removed
5 slices thin-slice whole
 wheat bread, crust removed
Mayonnaise

Beat cream cheese until light and fluffy; add 2 tablespoons whipping cream; beat well. Add onion and pimiento; mix well. Combine cheese spread and remaining whipping cream; beat well. Add olives.

Spread each bread slice with mayonnaise. Spread cream cheese mixture on 2 white bread slices; spread cheese spread mixture on 2 whole wheat bread slices. Stack slices alternately, cheese side up, beginning with white bread. Top with a slice of white bread, mayonnaise side down. Cut sandwich in half lengthwise and in 4 slices crosswise. Repeat procedure 4 times, using remaining bread slices and cheese mixtures. Yield: about 3½ dozen sandwiches.

VEGETABLES WITH BLUE CHEESE WHIP

3 pounds carrots, scraped,
 cut into 3-inch pieces, and
 sliced into thin strips
3 large bunches celery,
 cleaned, cut into 3-inch
 pieces, and sliced into thin
 strips
5 medium zucchini, sliced
3 large heads cauliflower,
 broken into flowerets
2 packages radishes, cut into
 roses
Blue Cheese Whip
Fresh watercress sprigs

Combine vegetables in a large crock or plastic container; cover with ice water. Chill.

Drain vegetables. Arrange on a large serving platter around a bowl of Blue Cheese Whip. Garnish with watercress sprigs. Yield: 48 servings.

Blue Cheese Whip:

2 cups (8 ounces) crumbled
 blue cheese
2 (16-ounce) cartons
 commercial sour cream,
 divided
¼ cup minced fresh
 watercress

Combine blue cheese and ½ cup sour cream; beat well. Fold in remaining sour cream and watercress. Cover and chill. Yield: 1½ quarts.

WEDDING PUNCH

1½ gallons water
6 cups sugar
1½ quarts freshly squeezed
 orange juice (about 1½
 dozen oranges)
2¼ cups freshly squeezed
 lemon juice (about 1½
 dozen lemons)
1 (46-ounce) can pineapple
 juice
2 (28-ounce) bottles ginger
 ale, chilled

Combine water and sugar in a large Dutch oven, stirring well. Bring to a boil. Reduce heat; cover and simmer until sugar dissolves. Remove from heat, and cool.

Combine freshly squeezed juice and pineapple juice. Stir into cooled sugar-water mixture. Pour mixture into freezer containers. Cover and freeze until solid.

Allow frozen juice mixture to thaw 2 hours prior to serving. Transfer partially frozen juice to punch bowl. Add chilled ginger ale just before serving; stir well. Yield: about 2½ gallons.

Dr. and Mrs. Victor Miller before departing on their honeymoon from Hagerstown, Maryland, on June 1, 1905.

SPIRITED GROOM'S CAKE

¾ cup butter or margarine, softened
3 cups sugar
3 eggs, separated
6 (1-ounce) squares unsweetened chocolate, melted
3 tablespoons bourbon whiskey
1½ teaspoons vanilla extract
3 cups sifted cake flour
1 tablespoon baking powder
¾ teaspoon salt
2¼ cups milk
1½ cups chopped pecans
Chocolate Bourbon Frosting

Cream butter in a large mixing bowl; gradually add sugar, beating well. Add egg yolks, one at a time, beating well after each addition. Add melted chocolate, bourbon, and vanilla; beat well.

Combine flour, baking powder, and salt in a medium mixing bowl; sift 3 times. Add to creamed mixture alternately with milk, beginning and ending with flour mixture. Stir well after each addition.

Beat egg whites (at room temperature) in a medium mixing bowl until soft peaks form. Fold into batter. Gently fold in pecans.

Pour batter evenly into a greased and waxed paper-lined 13- x 9- x 2-inch baking pan and a greased and waxed paper-lined 8-inch square baking pan. Bake at 350° for 35 minutes or until a wooden pick inserted in center comes out clean. Cool in pans 10 minutes; remove cakes from pans, and let cool completely on wire racks.

Spread top and sides of larger layer evenly with Chocolate Bourbon Frosting. Place smaller layer, bottom side down, in middle of frosted bottom layer. Spread top and sides of top layer evenly with Chocolate Bourbon Frosting. Decorate cake, as desired, with remaining frosting, using a pastry bag fitted with desired tips. Yield: one 13- x 9-inch layer cake.

Chocolate Bourbon Frosting:

1 cup butter or margarine, melted
2 (16-ounce) packages powdered sugar, sifted
¼ cup cocoa
About 1 cup whipping cream
2 tablespoons bourbon

Combine butter, sugar, and cocoa in a large mixing bowl; beat well. Add whipping cream as needed for desired spreading consistency. Stir in bourbon. Yield: frosting for one 13- x 9-inch layer cake.

EVENING ENTERTAINMENT

"Come over for games and dessert!" Mah-Jongg is "in" again. Orange Charlotte, Ice Cream Sandwiches, and Hot Chocolate — and a good bridge game — never left!

Glancing back at our earlier days, when colonials were hell-bent on mere survival, we are sometimes surprised to learn that they played as hard as they worked to stay alive. It was commonplace for men and women to take risks to attend a ball or other entertainments away from home. Carriages with lanterns traveled rude roadways in all weathers because the Southern temperament demanded a well-rounded social life. It has been truly said that the Southerner could not thrive without his quota of dancing and gaming. These pursuits are as surely a part of our heritage as is the food we call Southern.

A city like Savannah no sooner came into money than men turned out in tight broadcloth trousers and colorful evening coats and rode through streets of sand to attend balls where good music reigned from sunset 'til, sometimes, sunrise. Women were elegantly gowned and did not abstain from the omnipresent punch bowl. Every account of evening parties over the years, whether from balls, receptions, or suppers, details splendid food: A midnight supper would have included almonds, raisins, apples, oranges, jelly, candy, sugarplums, kisses, and cake. If we envision quail, venison, and wild duck, we err; those were daily fare.

The Southerners' love of dancing bordered on mania. At balls, they danced the minuet, but before the party ended, there would be country reels measured by fiddles and the French horn. Games were exceedingly popular. At fancy evening affairs, there were tables, cards, and board games for non-dancers. Charades was popular in colonial days and still entertains us at parties.

Each level of society, not just the gentry, had its own lively party forms. On the frontier, girls improvised their "ball gowns" by day and danced tirelessly all night. They wheeled through the maze of the "Republican Six-Reel" on the puncheon floor of a one-room cabin from which the furniture had been removed. Dinner would be served on a makeshift table of planks resting on stakes driven into the ground and consisted of a profusion of plain fare, but always represented the best the host could procure.

NAME YOUR GAME DESSERT PARTY

Since not everyone enjoys the same sorts of games, why not stage a party at which there is a choice for all? Offer board games and plenty of cards for bridge, canasta, and rummy. And no one can tell when Trivial Pursuit, constantly fortified with new subject matter, will run its course. Old-fashioned bunco has its following, and there's "42" as well — so get out the dominoes. There is one thing all gamesmen have in common: they are hungry and thirsty. Beverages will be needed throughout the evening, but the food can be served either before the games begin or during an intermission. Word of warning: game parties are addictive.

ORANGE CHARLOTTE
BUNCO BON BONS
ICE CREAM SANDWICHES
COFFEE OR HOT CHOCOLATE

Serves 8

ORANGE CHARLOTTE

1 envelope unflavored gelatin
¼ cup cold water
¼ cup hot water
¾ cup sugar
3 eggs, separated
1 teaspoon grated orange rind
1 cup orange juice
1 cup whipping cream
Additional whipping cream, whipped
Fresh orange slices or orange peel strips

Soften gelatin in cold water.
Combine water, sugar, and yolks in top of a double boiler. Cook over boiling water, stirring constantly, until thickened and bubbly. Remove from heat; stir in orange rind, juice, and softened gelatin. Cool to consistency of unbeaten egg whites.
Beat egg whites (at room temperature) until stiff peaks form. Fold into orange mixture. Beat 1 cup whipping cream until stiff peaks form. Fold into egg mixture. Spoon mixture evenly into parfait glasses. Chill thoroughly. Garnish with additional whipped cream and orange slices or orange peel strips. Yield: 8 servings.

If bunco is the name of your game, Bunco Bon Bons will make an impression.

Or if your foursome prefers bridge, try cutting cakes into hearts, clubs, and spades instead of dice.

BUNCO BON BONS

⅓ cup butter or margarine, softened
1 cup sugar
2 eggs
½ teaspoon baking soda
1 cup buttermilk
1½ cups all-purpose flour
½ cup cocoa
1 teaspoon baking powder
½ teaspoon salt
1 teaspoon vanilla extract
Seven-Minute Frosting
Semisweet chocolate morsels

Cream butter in a large mixing bowl; gradually add sugar, beating well. Add eggs; beat until well blended.

Dissolve soda in buttermilk; set aside.

Combine flour, cocoa, baking powder, and salt; sift 3 times. Add to creamed mixture alternately with reserved buttermilk mixture, beginning and ending with flour mixture; mix well. Stir in vanilla.

Pour batter into a greased and floured 9-inch square baking pan. Bake at 375° for 25 minutes or until a wooden pick inserted in center comes out clean. Remove cake from pan; cool on a wire rack.

Cut cake into 2-inch squares. Spread top and sides of each square with Seven-Minute Frosting. Garnish each with chocolate morsels to resemble dice. Yield: 8 servings.

Seven-Minute Frosting:

1½ cups sugar
2 egg whites
1 tablespoon light corn syrup
¼ teaspoon cream of tartar
¼ cup plus 1 tablespoon cold water
1 teaspoon vanilla extract

Combine sugar, egg whites (at room temperature), syrup, and cream of tartar in top of a large double boiler; add water, and beat at low speed of an electric mixer 30 seconds or just until blended.

Place over rapidly boiling water; beat constantly at high speed of electric mixer 7 minutes or until stiff peaks form. Remove from heat. Add vanilla; beat 2 to 3 minutes or until frosting is thick enough to spread. Yield: frosting for one 9-inch square cake.

ICE CREAM SANDWICHES

1 cup butter or margarine, softened
2 cups sugar
3 eggs
3 cups all-purpose flour
2 teaspoons baking powder
1 cup milk
1 teaspoon vanilla extract
1 (½-gallon) carton strawberry ice cream
Chocolate syrup

Cream butter; gradually add sugar, ¼ cup at a time, beating well. Add eggs; beat well.

Combine flour and baking powder, mixing well; add to creamed mixture alternately with milk, beginning and ending with flour mixture. Stir in vanilla.

Pour batter into 3 well-greased 7½- x 3- x 2-inch loaf-pans. Bake at 350° for 50 minutes or until a wooden pick inserted in center comes out clean. Cool in pans 10 minutes; remove loaves from pans, and cool completely on wire racks. Slice 2 loaves into ¼-inch-thick slices; the remaining loaf may be frozen for other uses.

Remove cardboard carton from ice cream. Slice block of ice cream in half lengthwise; slice each half crosswise into ⅜-inch slices. Place a slice of ice cream on half the cake slices; drizzle chocolate syrup over each. Top with remaining cake slices to form a sandwich. Cover and freeze until ready to serve. Yield: 8 servings.

"42" SUPPER PARTY

Texans never tire of the game they call "42," which is played with a set of dominoes. Any excuse for getting up a game is good, be it birthday, Arbor Day, or just "feel-like-a-party" day. Guests can be all men, all women, or a judicious mix; youngsters learn early. Along with the game, they pick up the fact that food is always served when "42" is played. Depending upon the time of day, a light supper served picnic-style may be in order. At times it will be lunch, or a group can gather after dinner for a game and a rich dessert. A rich dessert, in fact, is the common denominator. For this supper party: Chewy Blonde Brownies and ice cream.

FRIED CHICKEN
SOUTHERN BAKED BEANS
CREAMY FRUIT SALAD
CORNBREAD
CHEWY BLONDE BROWNIES
VANILLA ICE CREAM

Serves 12

FRIED CHICKEN

3 (3- to 3½-pound)
  broiler-fryers, cut up
1 tablespoon garlic powder
3 cups buttermilk
4½ cups self-rising flour
1 tablespoon salt
1½ teaspoons pepper
Vegetable oil

Sprinkle surface of chicken with garlic powder. Place chicken in shallow pans, and pour buttermilk over top. Cover; refrigerate at least 20 minutes.

Combine flour, salt, and pepper in a plastic or paper bag; shake to mix. Remove chicken from buttermilk; discard buttermilk. Place 2 to 3 pieces of chicken in bag, and shake well. Repeat procedure with remaining chicken.

Heat 1 inch of oil in a large skillet to 350°. Add chicken, and fry 25 minutes or until golden brown, turning once. Drain chicken well on paper towels. Yield: 12 servings.

For your "42" party:
Fried Chicken, Southern
Baked Beans, Creamy Fruit
Salad, and Cornbread.

SOUTHERN BAKED BEANS

1 bell pepper, seeded, sliced,
   and divided
1 medium onion, sliced and
   divided
3 (28-ounce) cans pork and
   beans, drained
¾ cup firmly packed brown
   sugar
1 (14-ounce) bottle catsup
2 tablespoons prepared
   mustard
3 slices bacon, halved

Combine bell pepper and onion in a 3-quart casserole, reserving 1 slice of each. Combine beans, sugar, catsup, and mustard; mix well. Pour into casserole. Place bacon on top of bean mixture. Bake, uncovered, at 350° for 1 hour. Reduce heat to 300°, and bake an additional hour. Garnish with reserved onion and bell pepper slices. Yield: 12 servings.

CREAMY FRUIT SALAD

1 envelope unflavored gelatin
¼ cup water
1 (30-ounce) can fruit
   cocktail, undrained
¼ cup mayonnaise
¼ cup maraschino cherry
   juice
½ cup whipping cream,
   whipped
Curly leaf lettuce
Maraschino cherries, halved

Combine gelatin and water in top of a double boiler; let stand 5 minutes. Cook over boiling water, stirring constantly, until gelatin dissolves. Remove from heat, and cool.

Combine fruit cocktail and mayonnaise; stir well. Add dissolved gelatin and maraschino cherry juice; mix well. Fold in whipped cream. Spoon mixture into 12 lightly oiled individual molds. Chill until firm.

Turn molds out onto lettuce-lined serving plates; garnish with cherry halves. Serve immediately. Yield: 12 servings.

Two young ladies entertain their beaus at a supper party, North Carolina, 1936.

CORNBREAD

2 cups cornmeal
½ cup all-purpose flour
¼ cup plus 2 tablespoons
   sugar
¾ teaspoon salt
1 teaspoon baking soda
2 cups buttermilk
2 eggs, well beaten
2 tablespoons butter or
   margarine, melted

Sift together cornmeal, flour, sugar, and salt in a large mixing bowl. Dissolve soda in buttermilk; add to cornmeal mixture, stirring well. Add eggs and melted butter; mix well.

Heat two well-greased 8-inch cast-iron skillets in a 400° oven for 3 minutes or until very hot. Pour batter evenly into hot skillets. Bake at 400° for 30 minutes or until lightly browned. Yield: 12 servings.

CHEWY BLONDE BROWNIES

½ cup butter or margarine,
   softened
2⅓ cups firmly packed brown
   sugar
4 eggs
1 teaspoon vanilla extract
2 cups all-purpose flour
2 teaspoons baking
   powder
¼ teaspoon salt
1½ cups chopped pecans
Additional all-purpose flour

Cream butter in a large mixing bowl; gradually add sugar, beating well. Add eggs, one at a time, beating well after each addition. Stir in vanilla.

Combine 2 cups flour, baking powder, and salt; add to creamed mixture, stirring until smooth. Dredge pecans in additional flour, and stir into batter. Pour batter into a lightly greased and floured 13- x 9- x 2-inch baking pan.

Bake at 350° for 40 minutes. Cool brownies completely in pan. Cut into 2-inch squares. Yield: about 2 dozen.

ATLANTA WELCOMES THE MET

Yesterday's lavish tradition of hospitality set the stage in 1910 when Atlanta first played host to the Metropolitan Opera. Parties barely allowed time to change apparel for the next performance. Grandiose entertainment honored Geraldine Farrar, the *grande dame* of opera who simultaneously shocked and charmed Atlantans with her dramatic temperament. Silver baskets filled with little cakes initialed "G.F." adorned a table; a bunch of "electric" grapes twinkled beside them; a hundred canary birds competed with the orchestra on the porch. Everything about the week of opera came in large sizes and can only be described in superlatives.

CHAFING DISH CRAB DIP
or
BLUE CHEESE MOUSSE
CURRIED SHRIMP IN RICE MOLD
GREEN BEANS WITH SOUR CREAM DRESSING
BROILED TOMATOES
PECAN TORTE
WHITE WINE * COFFEE

Serves 12

Music Division, New York Public Library at Lincoln Center, Astor, Lenox and Tilden Foundation

Metropolitan Opera star Geraldine Farrar in Tosca. *She captivated Atlanta.*

CHAFING DISH CRAB DIP

2 (8-ounce) packages cream
    cheese, softened
½ cup butter or margarine
½ cup half-and-half
1 tablespoon grated onion
1 tablespoon lemon juice
1 teaspoon Worcestershire
    sauce
⅛ teaspoon hot sauce
½ teaspoon salt
1 pound claw or lump
    crabmeat, drained and
    flaked
Melba toast

Combine cream cheese, butter, and half-and-half in top of a double boiler; cook over simmering water, stirring constantly, until mixture melts. Stir in onion, lemon juice, Worcestershire sauce, hot sauce, and salt.

Remove from heat, and fold in crabmeat. Transfer mixture to a chafing dish, and serve with melba toast. Yield: 4½ cups.

Blue Cheese Mousse is a tasty addition to a party. Garnish with grapes and ivy leaves.

BLUE CHEESE MOUSSE

2 eggs, separated
¼ cup half-and-half
1 envelope unflavored
   gelatin
¼ cup cold water
8 ounces blue cheese
1 cup whipping cream,
   whipped
Fresh grape clusters

Combine egg yolks and half-and-half in a small saucepan; stir until well blended. Cook over low heat, stirring constantly, until mixture coats a metal spoon. Immediately remove from heat, and set aside.

Soften gelatin in cold water in top of a double boiler. Cook over simmering water, stirring constantly, until gelatin dissolves. Remove from heat, and add to reserved egg yolk mixture. Set aside.

Crumble blue cheese in top of double boiler. Cook over simmering water, stirring constantly, until cheese melts. Fold into reserved gelatin mixture.

Beat egg whites (at room temperature) until stiff peaks form. Fold into blue cheese mixture. Gently fold in whipped cream.

Spoon mixture into a lightly oiled 1-quart mold. Cover and refrigerate overnight. Unmold mousse onto a serving platter, and garnish with grape clusters. Serve with assorted crackers or toast rounds. Yield: 12 appetizer servings.

CURRIED SHRIMP IN RICE MOLD

5 cups cooked white rice
3 chicken-flavored bouillon
   cubes
¼ cup boiling water
1 tablespoon curry
   powder
½ teaspoon salt
¼ teaspoon white pepper
3 tablespoons butter or
   margarine
3 tablespoons all-purpose
   flour
3 cups milk
1½ pounds small shrimp,
   cooked, peeled, and
   deveined
Paprika
3 hard-cooked eggs, cut into
   wedges
Fresh parsley sprigs

Pack hot cooked rice into an oiled 5-cup ring mold. Place mold in a shallow pan, and add water to pan to a depth of 1 inch. Bake at 350° for 15 minutes. Invert mold onto a warm serving platter. Set aside, and keep warm.

Dissolve bouillon cubes in boiling water. Stir in curry powder, salt, and pepper; set mixture aside.

Melt butter in a small Dutch oven over low heat; add flour, stirring until smooth. Cook 1 minute, stirring constantly. Gradually add milk and reserved bouillon mixture; cook over medium heat, stirring constantly, until thickened and bubbly. Remove from heat, and stir in shrimp.

Pour curried shrimp mixture into center of reserved rice ring. Sprinkle top with paprika. Garnish platter with egg wedges and parsley. Serve immediately. Yield: 12 servings.

Ad for a very robust breed of tomatoes, c.1890.

GREEN BEANS WITH SOUR CREAM DRESSING

4 (16-ounce) cans cut green beans, drained
2 medium onions, thinly sliced
½ cup vegetable oil
½ cup vinegar
1 teaspoon salt
½ teaspoon coarsely ground black pepper
Sour Cream Dressing
Lettuce leaves
Fresh parsley sprigs (optional)

Combine beans and onion in a shallow dish. Combine oil, vinegar, salt, and pepper in a jar with a tight-fitting lid; shake vigorously. Pour marinade over bean mixture. Cover; marinate in refrigerator at least 2 hours. Drain; discard onion.

Combine beans and Sour Cream Dressing; toss lightly. Chill thoroughly. Place in a lettuce-lined serving bowl, and garnish with parsley, if desired. Yield: 12 servings.

Sour Cream Dressing:

1 (8-ounce) carton commercial sour cream
½ cup mayonnaise
1 tablespoon prepared horseradish
1 teaspoon lemon juice
¼ teaspoon onion juice
¼ teaspoon dry mustard

Combine all ingredients in a small mixing bowl, stirring well. Cover and chill thoroughly. Yield: 1¾ cups.

BROILED TOMATOES

12 small firm tomatoes
Salt and pepper to taste
3 tablespoons butter or margarine, melted
⅓ cup seasoned, dry breadcrumbs
⅓ cup grated Parmesan cheese
2 tablespoons chopped fresh parsley
⅛ teaspoon red pepper

Cut ¼-inch from tops of tomatoes. Place in a greased 9-inch square baking pan; sprinkle with salt and pepper.

Combine butter, breadcrumbs, cheese, parsley, and red pepper; mix well. Spoon mixture evenly over each tomato. Cover and bake at 350° for 15 minutes or until tender. Uncover and broil until topping is lightly browned. Serve immediately. Yield: 12 servings.

PECAN TORTE

3 eggs, separated
1 cup sugar
1 teaspoon vanilla extract
1 cup sifted cake flour
1 teaspoon baking powder
1 cup chopped dates
1½ cups chopped pecans, divided
1 cup whipping cream

Beat egg yolks until thick and lemon colored. Add sugar and vanilla; beat well. Combine flour, baking powder, dates, and 1 cup pecans. Stir well to coat. Add to yolk mixture. Beat egg whites (at room temperature) until stiff peaks form. Fold into flour mixture.

Spoon batter evenly into 2 greased and waxed paper-lined 9-inch round cakepans. Bake at 375° for 20 minutes or until cake springs back when lightly touched. Cool in pans 10 minutes; remove layers, and cool completely on wire racks.

Beat whipping cream until stiff peaks form. Spread whipped cream between layers and on top of cake. Sprinkle remaining pecans over cake. Yield: one 2-layer cake.

BUFFET SUPPER IN MISSISSIPPI

The *New Dixie Cookbook*, 1895, opines that there are sociable occasions such as after-opera routs and ball parties when conventional suppers may be dispensed with in favor of buffets. Two dozen dishes are suggested as sufficient for a standing supper, and it is strongly suggested, if more guests are desired, that the tables must be laid and served in the usual manner. We must assume that entertainment in the nature of a cocktail party is meant. In Mississippi's antebellum towns where evenings are soft and Spanish moss casts a romantic veil over all sociability, you'll find this kind of buffet supper, along with a place to sit down.

SMOKED TURKEY BREAST
LEMON BROCCOLI SPEARS
FRESH FRUIT SALAD WITH CELERY SEED DRESSING
RISEN BISCUITS
FROZEN CHOCOLATE DESSERT
COFFEE

Serves 12

SMOKED TURKEY BREAST

½ pound hickory chips, soaked in water
1 (4- to 6-pound) turkey breast
Additional hickory chips, soaked in water

Prepare charcoal fire in a smoker; let burn 10 to 15 minutes. Drain water from hickory chips to fill water pan half full. Sprinkle hickory chips over gray-white coals. Place water pan in smoker. Heavily grease wire food rack, and place on highest shelf in smoker.

Rinse turkey thoroughly in cold water, and pat dry. Place turkey breast on food rack. Cover smoker with lid, and open vent slightly to keep smoke and air circulating. Smoke turkey 3 hours. Refill water pan; add additional briquettes and hickory chips, as needed. Cover and smoke an additional 4 hours. Transfer turkey breast to a serving platter. Let stand 15 minutes before carving. Yield: 12 servings.

Note: After smoking, turkey breast may be frozen in an oven bag. Thaw and reheat in oven bag when ready to use.

LEMON BROCCOLI SPEARS

3 pounds fresh broccoli
1 teaspoon salt
Phyllo-Pastry Basket
Lemon slices
½ cup butter, melted
Juice of 2 lemons

Trim off large leaves and tough ends of stalks. If stalks are large, peel off outer covering with vegetable peeler. Wash thoroughly. Cut stems lengthwise from end through green head to make spears.

Cover and cook broccoli in a small amount of boiling salted water 15 minutes or just until

tender. Drain broccoli, and transfer to Phyllo-Pastry Basket. Garnish with lemon slices. Set aside.

Combine melted butter and lemon juice; serve immediately with broccoli spears. Yield: 12 servings.

Phyllo-Pastry Basket:

9 phyllo pastry sheets
½ cup butter, melted

Brush 8 phyllo sheets lightly with melted butter, and layer, butter sides up. Trim edges to make a 14- x 9-inch rectangle. Scallop edges of rectangle, using a 2-inch round cutter; trim excess pastry. Fit into a 10- x 6- x 2-inch baking dish to form a basket. Set aside.

Brush remaining phyllo sheet liberally with melted butter. Starting at short end, roll up jellyroll fashion, and curve roll to form a handle to fit a 6-inch-wide basket; place on a baking sheet. Bake basket and handle at 350° for 10 minutes or until golden brown. Let cool completely, and remove basket from dish. Carefully set each end of handle into basket, and secure with wooden picks. Set aside until ready to use. Yield: one 10- x 6-inch pastry basket.

View of antebellum Vicksburg, Mississippi.

FRESH FRUIT SALAD WITH CELERY SEED DRESSING

2 oranges, peeled, sectioned, and seeded
1 banana, peeled and sliced
½ pound white seedless grapes, halved
1 pint fresh strawberries, hulled and sliced
2 medium apples, unpeeled and sliced
2 kiwis, peeled and sliced
Lettuce leaves
Celery Seed Dressing

Arrange fruit on a lettuce-lined serving platter. Chill until ready to use. Serve salad with Celery Seed Dressing. Yield: 12 servings.

Note: Fruit may be tossed gently and placed in a lettuce-lined serving bowl. Chill until ready to serve.

Celery Seed Dressing:

½ cup sugar
⅓ cup honey
¼ cup vinegar
1 tablespoon lemon juice
1 teaspoon grated onion
¼ teaspoon salt
1 teaspoon celery seeds
1 teaspoon dry mustard
1 teaspoon paprika
1 cup vegetable oil

Combine all ingredients except oil in container of an electric blender; process until smooth. Continue processing while slowly adding oil in a steady stream. Cover and chill thoroughly. Yield: about 2 cups.

RISEN BISCUITS

1 package dry yeast
¼ cup warm water (105° to 115°)
5 cups all-purpose flour
1 tablespoon sugar
1 teaspoon salt
2 cups milk, scalded
¼ cup plus 2 tablespoons butter or margarine

Dissolve yeast in warm water, stirring well. Let stand 5 minutes or until bubbly. Set aside.

Combine flour, sugar, and salt in a large mixing bowl. Pour scalded milk over butter in a medium mixing bowl; stir until butter melts. Cool to lukewarm (105° to 115°). Add to flour mixture; stir well. Stir in dissolved yeast. Cover and refrigerate overnight.

Turn dough out onto a heavily floured surface, and knead 4 to 5 minutes. Roll to ¾-inch thickness; cut with a 1½-inch biscuit cutter.

Place biscuits in greased 13- x 9- x 2-inch baking pans. Cover and let rise 20 minutes or until doubled in bulk. Bake at 400° for 12 minutes or until lightly browned. Yield: about 3½ dozen.

FROZEN CHOCOLATE DESSERT

1 (6-ounce) package semisweet chocolate morsels
2 cups plus 2 tablespoons whipping cream, divided
4 eggs, separated
⅓ cup sifted powdered sugar
2 teaspoons vanilla extract, divided
½ cup sifted powdered sugar
1 dozen almond macaroons, crumbled and divided
½ cup finely chopped pecans
Whipped cream
12 maraschino cherries

Place chocolate and 2 tablespoons whipping cream in top of a double boiler; cook over simmering water, stirring constantly, until chocolate melts. Beat egg yolks until light and lemon colored; add beaten yolks and ⅓ cup sugar to chocolate mixture, stirring constantly, until mixture thickens. Remove from heat. Cool; stir in 1 teaspoon vanilla.

Beat egg whites (at room temperature) until stiff peaks form. Stir ½ cup egg whites into chocolate mixture; fold in remaining egg whites.

Beat 2 cups whipping cream until foamy; add ½ cup sugar, beating until soft peaks form. Stir in remaining vanilla.

Sprinkle half of macaroon crumbs into a 12- x 8- x 2-inch baking dish. Spoon half of chocolate mixture over crumbs. Spread sweetened whipped cream over chocolate. Spoon remaining chocolate over whipped cream. Sprinkle remaining macaroon crumbs and pecans over surface. Cover and freeze.

Remove from freezer; let stand 10 minutes. Cut into 3-inch squares. Garnish with additional whipped cream and cherries. Yield: 12 servings.

Fresh Fruit Salad (front) complements in color and taste the Smoked Turkey Breast, Lemon Broccoli, and Risen Biscuits.

DIXIELAND AFTER FIVE

In colonial days, liquor-related taxes ranked in notoriety along with tea-related taxes. It was not only in the South that drinking was defense against hardship and illness. Fiery punch, free-flowing rum, and wines fortified the new Americans and sometimes did lead to over-indulgence (duels were commonplace).

Some writers called it dissipation. Once the hardships were alleviated, however, the South settled comfortably and naturally into a relaxed attitude toward drinking. Nothing is more delightful in all Dixieland than our cocktail party, with its delicious array of dainty morsels offered as complements to an assortment of drinks.

ROQUEFORT ROLL
CHEESE BRAMBLES
HOT PEPPER PECANS
STUFFED MUSHROOMS
KRAUT BALLS
COLD MEAT TRAY
BARBECUED SHRIMP

Serves 24

Enjoying a musical evening at home, c.1907.

ROQUEFORT ROLL

2 (3-ounce) packages cream
  cheese, softened
1 (4-ounce) package
  Roquefort or blue cheese,
  softened
⅓ cup finely chopped green
  pepper
⅓ cup finely chopped celery
  hearts
1 tablespoon minced
  pimiento-stuffed olives
1 tablespoon finely chopped
  fresh parsley
Salt and pepper to taste
¾ cup finely chopped pecans

Combine cheese in a small
mixing bowl, and cream until
smooth. Add next 5 ingredients;
stir well.

Shape mixture into a log; roll
in chopped pecans. Chill several
hours. Transfer to a serving
platter; serve with crackers.
Yield: 24 appetizer servings.

CHEESE BRAMBLES

1 cup butter
2 (3-ounce) packages cream
  cheese, softened
2 cups all-purpose flour
1 teaspoon salt
⅛ teaspoon red pepper
½ cup (2 ounces) sharp
  Cheddar cheese, cut into
  ¼-inch cubes

Cream butter and cream
cheese in a large mixing bowl;
gradually stir in flour, salt, and
pepper, mixing until well
blended. Shape dough into 2
balls. Cover and chill at least 2
hours.

Work with one ball at a time.
Turn dough out onto a floured
surface. Roll to ⅛-inch thickness; cut into 2-inch squares.
Place a Cheddar cheese cube in
center of each square. Fold
squares in half diagonally to
form triangles. Press edges together with tines of a fork to
seal, and place on ungreased
baking sheets. Bake at 450° for
8 to 10 minutes. Repeat procedure with remaining dough and
Cheddar cheese. Serve hot.
Yield: 4 dozen.

HOT PEPPER PECANS

½ cup butter or margarine,
  melted
2 teaspoons soy sauce
½ teaspoon hot sauce
½ teaspoon salt
1 quart pecan halves

Combine butter, soy sauce,
hot sauce, and salt in a large
mixing bowl, mixing until well
blended; add pecans, stirring to
coat well.

Spread pecans in a single
layer in a 13- x 9- x 2-inch baking pan. Bake at 300°, stirring
frequently, 20 minutes or until
pecans are crisp; drain on paper
towels. Cool completely, and
store in airtight containers
until ready to serve. Yield: 1
quart.

STUFFED MUSHROOMS

48 medium-size fresh
  mushrooms (about 1½
  pounds)
3 green onions, finely
  chopped
¼ cup butter or
  margarine
1 egg, well beaten
½ cup seasoned, dry
  breadcrumbs
3 tablespoons grated
  Parmesan cheese
1 tablespoon chopped fresh
  parsley
¼ teaspoon salt
Dash of pepper
Paprika

Remove stems from mush-
rooms; chop stems. Set mushroom caps aside.

Sauté mushroom stems and
onion in butter in a small saucepan until tender; remove from
heat. Stir in next 6 ingredients.
Spoon mixture into mushroom
caps; sprinkle with paprika.
Place in a 15- x 10- x 1-inch jellyroll pan. Bake at 450° for 8
minutes. Serve warm. Yield: 24
appetizer servings.

Note: Mushrooms may be prepared several hours in advance
and stored in refrigerator until
ready to bake.

KRAUT BALLS

½ pound mild bulk pork
  sausage
¼ cup chopped onion
1 (16-ounce) can chopped
  sauerkraut, drained
1 cup plus 2 tablespoons fine,
  dry breadcrumbs, divided
1 (3-ounce) package cream
  cheese, softened
2 tablespoons chopped fresh
  parsley
¼ cup plus 1 teaspoon
  prepared mustard, divided
¼ teaspoon garlic salt
⅛ teaspoon pepper
1 cup mayonnaise
2 eggs
¼ cup milk
½ cup all-purpose flour
Vegetable oil

Combine sausage and onion
in a large skillet; cook until sausage is browned, stirring to
crumble meat. Drain well. Add
sauerkraut and 2 tablespoons
breadcrumbs, mixing well.

Combine cream cheese, parsley, 1 teaspoon mustard, garlic
salt, and pepper in a large mixing bowl; mix well. Add sausage
mixture, mixing well. Cover and
chill thoroughly.

Combine mayonnaise and remaining mustard in a small
mixing bowl, stirring well; set
aside.

Combine eggs and milk in a
small mixing bowl; beat well.
Set aside.

Shape sausage mixture into
¾-inch balls; roll in flour. Dip
each ball in reserved egg mixture; roll in remaining breadcrumbs. Fry, a few at a time, in
deep, hot oil (375°) 2 minutes or
until golden brown. Drain on
paper towels. Serve warm with
reserved mayonnaise mixture.
Yield: about 5 dozen.

Note: Kraut Balls may be
made ahead of time and frozen.
To reheat, place a single layer in
a 13- x 9- x 2-inch baking pan,
and bake at 375° for 10 minutes
or until thoroughly heated.

Cold Meat Tray also holds cheeses, dill slices, and a tangy Mustard Spread to serve with cocktails.

BARBECUED SHRIMP

7 slices bacon
1 pound uncooked medium
  shrimp, peeled and deveined
1 tablespoon lemon juice
1 teaspoon Worcestershire
  sauce
⅛ teaspoon pepper
2 tablespoons butter or
  margarine
Barbecue Sauce
¼ cup chopped green onion
6 fresh mushrooms, sliced

Cut each bacon slice into 4 pieces; wrap each shrimp with a piece of bacon, and secure with a wooden pick. Place bacon-wrapped shrimp in a 10- x 8- x 2-inch baking dish. Sprinkle with lemon juice, Worcestershire sauce, and pepper; dot with butter. Brush liberally with Barbecue Sauce. Garnish top with chopped green onion and mushroom slices.

Bake at 425° for 20 minutes. Serve immediately. Yield: 24 appetizer servings.

Barbecue Sauce:

¼ cup water
2 tablespoons vinegar
3 tablespoons butter or
  margarine
¼ cup plus 2 tablespoons
  chopped onion
1 tablespoon sugar
1½ teaspoons Dijon mustard
½ teaspoon salt
⅛ teaspoon pepper
⅛ teaspoon red pepper
¼ cup plus 2 tablespoons
  catsup
1 tablespoon Worcestershire
  sauce

Combine first 9 ingredients in a medium saucepan, stirring well. Bring to a boil. Reduce heat; simmer, uncovered, 20 minutes. Remove from heat, and stir in remaining ingredients. Use immediately, or cover and store in refrigerator. Yield: about 1 cup.

COLD MEAT TRAY

3 pounds thinly sliced Swiss
  cheese
2 pounds thinly sliced,
  cooked ham
2 pounds thinly sliced,
  cooked roast beef
2 pounds thinly sliced,
  cooked turkey
1 (16-ounce) loaf thin-sliced
  rye bread
1 (16-ounce) loaf thin-sliced
  whole wheat bread
1 (16-ounce) jar sliced dill
  pickles, drained
Lettuce leaves
Mustard Spread

Arrange first 7 ingredients on a lettuce-lined serving platter. Serve with Mustard Spread. Yield: 24 servings.

Mustard Spread:

2 cups mayonnaise
2 tablespoons prepared
  mustard
1 tablespoon cider vinegar
Dash of pepper

Combine all ingredients in a small mixing bowl, and mix well. Chill thoroughly. Yield: about 2 cups.

COCKTAIL BUFFET AT THE
FIRST WHITE HOUSE OF THE CONFEDERACY

When Jefferson Davis became President of the Confederacy, the Provisional Congress purchased an official residence for him in Montgomery, Alabama, a modest frame home built by William Sayre in the 1830s. Although the Davises lived there only during the spring of 1861, Varina Davis made a profound impression on Montgomery society. The First White House of the Confederacy, overseen by the White House Association, is open to the public and is sometimes used for parties such as this cocktail buffet. The Gingersnaps came from a Davis family recipe, but Jeff Davis Punch was concocted by daughter Winnie for her father's birthday.

GAZPACHO TARTS
CURRIED SHRIMP PUFFS
BLACK-EYED PEA PÂTÉ
SWEET POTATO BISCUITS WITH BAKED HAM
COCONUT MACAROONS
GINGERSNAPS
PULLED SUGAR MINTS
JEFF DAVIS PUNCH

Serves 20

First White House of the Confederacy, Montgomery, Alabama.

GAZPACHO TARTS

3 medium tomatoes, peeled and quartered
1 cucumber, peeled and quartered
1 medium-size green pepper, seeded and quartered
1 large carrot, scraped and cut into 2-inch pieces
1 small onion, quartered
1 cup mayonnaise
1 teaspoon salt
1 teaspoon paprika
½ teaspoon dry mustard
1 teaspoon Worcestershire sauce
2 packages unflavored gelatin
½ cup cold water
Tart Shells (page 80)
Cucumber and carrot slices

Process tomato, cucumber, green pepper, carrot, and onion in container of an electric blender until smooth. Combine mixture with mayonnaise, salt, paprika, mustard, and Worcestershire sauce; stir well.

Combine gelatin and cold water in a small saucepan; cook over low heat, stirring constantly, until gelatin dissolves. Add to tomato mixture, stirring well. Chill thoroughly.

Spoon 1 tablespoon filling into each Tart Shell; garnish with cucumber and carrot slices. Yield: about 6 dozen.

CURRIED SHRIMP PUFFS

½ cup butter
1 cup boiling water
1 cup all-purpose flour
½ teaspoon salt
½ teaspoon curry powder
1 teaspoon grated onion
4 eggs
2 cups finely chopped, cooked shrimp

Combine butter and boiling water in a medium saucepan; bring to a boil. Add flour, salt, curry powder, and onion; cook, stirring vigorously over medium heat until mixture leaves sides of pan and forms a smooth ball. Remove from heat, and cool slightly.

Add eggs, one at a time, beating well after each addition; beat until batter is smooth. Fold in shrimp.

Drop batter by teaspoonfuls onto greased baking sheets. Bake at 450° for 10 minutes; reduce heat to 325°, and continue baking 10 minutes or until puffed and golden brown. Serve immediately. Yield: about 5 dozen.

BLACK-EYED PEA PÂTÉ

2 (16-ounce) cans black-eyed peas, undrained
2 envelopes unflavored gelatin
3 medium tomatoes, finely chopped
3 green onions, finely chopped
⅓ cup catsup
¼ cup mayonnaise
10 dashes hot sauce
1 teaspoon salt
Lettuce leaves
Cherry tomatoes (optional)

Drain peas, reserving liquid; set liquid aside. Process 2 cups peas in container of an electric blender until smooth. Set aside.

Soften gelatin in reserved liquid in a small saucepan. Cook over low heat, stirring constantly, until gelatin dissolves.

Combine next 6 ingredients in a large mixing bowl. Stir in pureed peas, whole peas, and gelatin mixture. Add enough water to yield 2 quarts. Pour pea mixture into a lightly oiled 8-cup mold. Chill until firm.

Unmold onto a lettuce-lined serving plate. Garnish with cherry tomatoes, if desired. Yield: 20 servings.

SWEET POTATO BISCUITS WITH BAKED HAM

3 cups all-purpose flour
2 tablespoons sugar
2 teaspoons baking powder
½ teaspoon baking soda
Dash of salt
¼ cup shortening
¾ cup mashed, cooked sweet potatoes
1 cup buttermilk
Baked ham slices

Combine flour, sugar, baking powder, soda, and salt in a large mixing bowl; stir well. Cut in shortening with a pastry blender until mixture resembles coarse meal. Stir in sweet potatoes. Add buttermilk, stirring with a fork until dry ingredients are moistened.

Turn dough out onto a lightly floured surface, and knead 4 to 5 times. Roll to ½-inch thickness; cut with a 1½-inch biscuit cutter. Place biscuits on a lightly greased baking sheet. Bake at 450° for 8 to 10 minutes or until lightly browned. Serve hot with baked ham. Yield: about 2½ dozen.

From the Black-eyed Pea Pâté, clockwise: Gazpacho Tarts, Sweet Potato Biscuits with Ham. And Jeff Davis Punch.

Varina Davis, First Lady of the Confederacy.

GINGERSNAPS

¾ cup shortening
1 cup sugar
1 egg
¼ cup molasses
2 cups all-purpose flour
1½ teaspoons baking soda
1½ teaspoons ground ginger
Additional sugar

Cream shortening in a large mixing bowl; gradually add 1 cup sugar, beating until light and fluffy. Add egg and molasses; beat well.

Sift together flour, soda, and ginger in a small mixing bowl; add to creamed mixture, stirring well. Shape dough into ½-inch balls, and roll in additional sugar.

Place balls 2 inches apart on greased cookie sheets. Bake at 350° for 10 minutes. Remove from cookie sheets; cool on wire racks. Store in airtight containers. Yield: about 4 dozen.

When Jefferson Davis married Varina Howell, he was 37. He had spent the previous 10 years living quietly on his Mississippi farm since the tragic early death of his first wife, the daughter of Colonel Zachary Taylor. The First White House of the Confederacy in Montgomery became a place of glamorous hospitality during Varina's brief tenure of 1861. The capital was moved to Richmond in 1862, but Varina and her family are still a proud part of Alabama's past. Their home is beautifully restored and furnished as graciously as when Varina herself held lavish dinners in that splendid dining room. Open to the public, it is one of the places Southerners hold most dear as a symbol of another era.

COCONUT MACAROONS

1 cup sugar, divided
2 tablespoons water
2 egg whites
¼ teaspoon salt
½ teaspoon vanilla extract
1 cup grated coconut

Combine ¾ cup sugar and water in a large saucepan. Bring to a boil over medium heat, stirring constantly. Continue to cook, without stirring, until mixture reaches soft ball stage (234°). (Wash down sides of saucepan frequently with a wet pastry brush to prevent sugar from crystallizing.) Remove from heat, and set aside.

Beat egg whites (at room temperature) in a medium mixing bowl until foamy. Add salt and vanilla, and continue beating until soft peaks form. Pour hot sugar mixture in a very thin stream into beaten egg whites while beating constantly at high speed of electric mixer. Continue to beat until mixture cools. Fold in grated coconut.

Drop mixture by heaping teaspoonfuls onto parchment-lined cookie sheets. Bake at 275° for 35 minutes or until lightly browned. Cool slightly on cookie sheets; gently remove from parchment, and cool completely on wire racks. Store in airtight containers. Yield: about 6 dozen.

PULLED SUGAR MINTS

4 cups sugar
2 cups water
½ teaspoon cream of tartar
Liquid food coloring
3 drops peppermint oil

Brush a marble slab with oil; place on a rack extended from an open oven heated to 200°.

Combine sugar, water, and cream of tartar in a large Dutch oven; stir well until dry ingredients dissolve. Cover and cook over medium-high heat 3 minutes to remove crystals from sides of pan. Uncover and continue to cook, without stirring, until mixture reaches hard crack stage (300°). Remove from heat, and stir in desired amount of food coloring.

Pour mixture slowly onto prepared marble slab; remain near heat source. (Any excess syrup may be placed in a greased pan on another oven rack until ready to use.) Sprinkle peppermint oil over hot mixture. Let cool briefly until skin begins to form. Work edges of mixture into center mass, using a well-greased metal spatula. Continue flipping edges into center mass until mixture mounds into a ball.

Pick up ball with oiled fingers or well-greased rubber gloves. Working near source of heat, stretch candy 18 inches between hands; fold ends together. Stretch and fold again. Repeat stretching and folding procedure 10 minutes or until candy becomes opaque.

Pull a small portion of candy into ½-inch-wide strips; curl each strip back and forth accordion fashion, or cut with well-greased kitchen shears to desired sizes. Let cool. Yield: about 4 dozen mints.

JEFF DAVIS PUNCH

3½ cups sugar
3½ cups water
1½ cups lemon juice
6 (750 ml) bottles Burgundy or other dry red wine, chilled
1 (750 ml) bottle dry sherry, chilled
2 cups light rum
1 cup brandy
Ice ring
3 (33.8-ounce) bottles club soda, chilled
3 (28-ounce) bottles ginger ale, chilled
Cucumber slices
Orange slices

Combine sugar, water, and lemon juice in a large crock or plastic container; stir until sugar dissolves. Add next four ingredients, stirring well.

Pour half the wine mixture into a large punch bowl over ice ring; stir in half the club soda and ginger ale. Add cucumber and orange slices to punch bowl. Add wine mixture, club soda, and ginger ale to replenish bowl as needed. Yield: about 7 gallons.

Engraved portrait of Jefferson Davis, President of the Confederacy.

ON THE GRAND SCALE

Many of the South's galas are the work of committees and have been since before the citizenry of Alexandria, Virginia, planned a Birth Night Ball and Entertainment in honor of George Washington. Dolley Madison, famous for such innovative social gatherings as her "Drawing Rooms," really was a committee of one — with a chef and dozens of willing hands to attend to details. A large soiree is scarcely manageable single-handed, even by the most energetic hostess.

The meaning of the New Orleans Soiree as a training ground for the young in the social graces widened to cover just about any fancy get-together, such as the germans, so much the rage in the late 1800s, especially in debutante circles. They continued to be popular into the 1900s. At some Southern universities, men's german clubs sponsored regular dances. The term german simply denotes a dance or ball. The men were not, unless incidentally, German; nor were they united by scholarship in the German language.

Since the days of Captain John Smith at Jamestown, the South has drawn heavily on the military for its heroes, even sending some of them to the presidency. Grand scale celebrations for two such men are included here. Alexandria was but one city to honor a president in such a way. The St. Augustine story shows how fondly Florida remembered General Andrew Jackson. We may wonder why a Hermitage Ball and Supper came to be given at St. Augustine, Florida. Upon hearing that money was needed to restore the run-down Hermitage, Henry Flagler offered the luxurious Ponce de León for a great ball and supper. George Mortimer Pullman of the Pullman Palace Car Company placed a fine sleeper at the disposal of the guests coming from great distances. The presidents of Mexico and the United States sent representatives. Cost of tickets? Five dollars per couple.

The romantic ideal of the man in uniform lives on at the Naval Academy at Annapolis. The Ring Dance and ceremony highlights the lives of the men and their sweethearts. At parties on so grand a scale, thousands may be served. The trick is to make each helping taste one-of-a-kind.

MENU OF MENUS

NEW ORLEANS SOIREE

SOIREE AT PARKHURST

DOLLEY MADISON'S DRAWING ROOM

SATURDAY NIGHT GERMANS IN SAVANNAH

ANNAPOLIS RING DANCE AND BANQUET

GEORGE WASHINGTON'S BIRTH NIGHT CELEBRATION

THE HERMITAGE BALL AND SUPPER IN ST. AUGUSTINE

Scotch Pancakes with fresh fruit (front); scoops of Pistachio Ice Cream in silver stand; Cranberry Syrup and Refreshing Lemonade to quaff with Vanilla Wafers (right).

111

NEW ORLEANS SOIREE

The courtly manners of old-line Louisiana Creole men and women were so deeply ingrained and so natural they seemed to have been inborn. Not quite, but their training began early, by way of parties known as soirees given by their parents. Soirees were held in private homes; guest youngsters were escorted by their fathers.

The host parents served simple, light refreshments. "Sirops" and lemonade accompanied small cakes, wafers, and fruits. As the evening progressed, fathers enjoyed more strengthening libations and admired their children shamelessly. In the wee hours, coffee, chocolate, and sometimes cups of consommé were passed.

SCOTCH PANCAKES
ASSORTED FRESH FRUIT
VANILLA WAFERS
PISTACHIO ICE CREAM
HOT CHOCOLATE
CRANBERRY SYRUP
REFRESHING LEMONADE
COFFEE

Serves 20

SCOTCH PANCAKES

¼ cup butter or margarine
½ cup sifted powdered sugar
1 egg
1 cup all-purpose flour
2 teaspoons baking powder
¼ teaspoon baking soda
⅔ cup milk

Cream butter in a medium mixing bowl; gradually add sugar, beating well. Add egg; beat well.

Combine flour, baking powder, and soda; stir well. Add to creamed mixture alternately with milk, beginning and ending with flour mixture.

Drop batter by heaping teaspoonfuls onto a hot, lightly greased griddle or skillet. Cook until tops of pancakes are covered with bubbles and edges appear slightly dry. Turn and continue cooking until bottom sides are browned. Serve hot or cold. Yield: about 3½ dozen.

Festive foursome lift a toast as part of an evening of celebration, c.1900.

VANILLA WAFERS

⅓ cup shortening
1 cup sugar
1 egg
2 cups all-purpose flour
2 teaspoons baking powder
½ teaspoon salt
¼ cup milk
2 teaspoons vanilla extract

Cream shortening in a medium mixing bowl; gradually add sugar, beating well. Add egg; beat well.

Combine flour, baking powder, and salt; stir well. Add to creamed mixture alternately with milk, beginning and ending with flour mixture. Stir in vanilla. Chill.

Divide dough into fourths. Working with one portion of dough at a time, turn dough out onto a lightly floured surface, and roll to ¼-inch thickness. Cut with a floured 1½-inch round cookie cutter. Place 2 inches apart on greased cookie sheets. Bake at 375° for 8 minutes or until lightly browned. Cool slightly on cookie sheets; remove to wire racks to cool completely. Repeat procedure with remaining dough. Yield: about 7 dozen.

Delicious Cranberry Syrup.

PISTACHIO ICE CREAM

1½ quarts half-and-half, divided
1½ cups sugar
3 egg yolks, beaten
1 cup finely chopped pistachio nuts
1 tablespoon almond extract
5 to 6 drops green food coloring

Scald 3 cups half-and-half in a saucepan; stir in sugar. Cook over low heat, stirring constantly, until sugar dissolves.

Gradually stir one-fourth of hot mixture into beaten egg yolks; add to remaining hot mixture, stirring constantly. Remove from heat; stir in pistachios. Let cool to room temperature. Stir in remaining half-and-half, almond extract, and food coloring.

Pour mixture into freezer can of a 1-gallon hand-turned or electric freezer. Freeze according to manufacturer's instructions. Let ripen at least 1½ to 2 hours before serving. Scoop ice cream into individual bowls, and serve immediately. Yield: about 3 quarts.

HOT CHOCOLATE

1 gallon milk
2 (4-ounce) bars sweet baking chocolate
1 cup sugar
2 teaspoons vanilla extract
½ teaspoon salt
Whipped cream

Cook milk in a large Dutch oven over medium heat until milk is warm.

Cook chocolate in top of a double boiler over simmering water, stirring constantly, until chocolate melts slightly. Gradually add 1 cup warm milk, stirring constantly, until chocolate melts completely. Stir chocolate milk mixture into remaining warm milk. Add sugar, vanilla, and salt; continue to cook, stirring constantly, until sugar dissolves and milk is thoroughly heated.

Pour hot chocolate into mugs, and top each with a dollop of whipped cream. Serve immediately. Yield: about 1 gallon.

CRANBERRY SYRUP

8 cups sugar
1½ quarts water
2 cups cranberry juice cocktail
1 teaspoon lemon juice
Shaved ice

Combine sugar and water in a large Dutch oven; stir well. Cook over medium heat until mixture reaches 220°. Stir in cranberry juice cocktail and lemon juice. Continue to cook over medium heat 5 minutes. Remove from heat, and let cool.

Pour syrup into bottles, and chill. Pour chilled syrup over shaved ice in glasses to serve. Yield: about 2 quarts.

REFRESHING LEMONADE

1½ quarts freshly squeezed lemon juice (about 4 dozen lemons)
6 quarts water
3¾ cups sugar
Lemon slices

Combine all ingredients, except lemon slices in a large container, stirring well. Chill thoroughly.

Serve over ice, and garnish with lemon slices. Yield: about 2 gallons.

Auguste Edouart's detailed silhouette of an 1840 reception.

SOIREE AT PARKHURST

The pleasure of Mr. G. Cheston, Jr. and Lady's Company is respectfully requested at PARKHURST, on Tuesday, 11th inst., at 5 p.m.; the Dancing will commence at 8 p.m. West River, August 3rd, 1857." Eight men gave the soiree at magnificent Parkhurst in Harwood, Maryland. A treasury of the most elegant foods would have been served. The original invitation to Mr. Cheston now hangs in the dining room, which was designated the ballroom when Richard Mercer, grandson of John Francis Mercer (tenth governor of Maryland), supervised construction of the main part in 1848. Kitchen and family room comprise the original building, which dates back to the Revolutionary War and at one time served as a girls' school.

CRAB CROQUETTES
HAM AND CHEESE TOAST ROUNDS
STUFFED PORK TENDERLOINS
DRESSED CUCUMBERS WITH TOMATOES
BRUSSELS SPROUTS
PETITE BRIOCHE
MRS. HOWARD'S TRIFLE
ORANGE ICE
CHERRY BOUNCE

CLARET CUP * QUEEN'S PUNCH

Serves 12 to 15

CRAB CROQUETTES

1 egg, well beaten
½ cup soft breadcrumbs
¼ cup mayonnaise
¼ cup finely chopped green
   pepper
2 teaspoons Worcestershire
   sauce
1 teaspoon lemon juice
1 teaspoon dry mustard
½ teaspoon salt
⅛ teaspoon white pepper
1 pound lump or flake
   crabmeat, drained
Vegetable oil
Lemon wedges
Cocktail sauce

Combine first 9 ingredients in a medium mixing bowl; mix well. Gently fold in crabmeat.

Shape mixture into 2- x 1-inch croquettes. Heat ¼ inch oil in a large skillet over medium-high heat. Cook croquettes 3 minutes on each side or until golden brown. Drain well on paper towels. Serve immediately with lemon wedges and cocktail sauce. Yield: 1½ dozen.

HAM AND CHEESE TOAST ROUNDS

12 slices bread
1 egg, beaten
⅓ cup mayonnaise
1 cup (4 ounces) shredded
   Swiss cheese
½ teaspoon Worcestershire
   sauce
⅛ teaspoon dry mustard
Dash of pepper
6 drops hot sauce
1 cup finely chopped, cooked
   ham
Paprika

Cut 2 rounds from each bread slice, using a 2-inch biscuit cutter. Toast rounds on both sides.

Combine egg, mayonnaise, cheese, Worcestershire sauce, mustard, pepper, and hot sauce; mix well. Stir in ham. Spread toast rounds evenly with ham mixture; sprinkle each lightly with paprika. Place rounds on a 15- x 10- x 1-inch jellyroll pan. Bake at 350° for 12 minutes or until lightly browned. Yield: 2 dozen.

STUFFED PORK TENDERLOINS

8 dried pitted prunes
1½ cups water, divided
2 (1½- to 2-pound) pork
   tenderloins
1 teaspoon salt, divided
2 cooking apples, peeled,
   cored, chopped, and divided
1 cup whipping cream
1 (8-ounce) carton
   commercial sour cream
2 tablespoons white wine
¼ teaspoon white pepper
3 tablespoons butter or
   margarine
¼ cup all-purpose flour
Fresh parsley sprigs
Apple slices

Combine prunes and 1 cup water in a small saucepan; cover and let stand at room temperature overnight. Bring prune mixture to a boil. Reduce heat, and simmer 10 minutes. Drain prunes; coarsely chop, and set aside.

Cut tenderloins almost in half lengthwise; open and pound to ¼-inch thickness. Sprinkle each tenderloin with ¼ teaspoon salt. Place half of apples and reserved prunes evenly over each tenderloin. Roll up each tenderloin jellyroll fashion; tie each end with kitchen string.

Combine whipping cream, sour cream, wine, remaining salt, and pepper in a medium mixing bowl, stirring well. Set aside.

Brown pork rolls on all sides in butter in a large skillet. Pour reserved whipping cream mixture over browned rolls. Cover and simmer 1½ hours. Remove rolls to a warm serving platter; set aside.

Combine flour and remaining water; stir into hot mixture in skillet, using a wire whisk. Cook over low heat, stirring constantly, until thickened. Pour over rolls; garnish with parsley sprigs and apple slices. Yield: 12 to 15 servings.

Stuffed Pork Tenderloin, Brussels Sprouts, Petite Brioche.

Collection of Kit Barry, Brattleboro, Vermont

After Dinner Tricks & Puzzles WITH YOUR SEAL BRAND COFFEE

COMPLIMENTS OF CHASE & SANBORN

Chase and Sanborn published this book promoting Seal Brand Coffee for parties, 1896.

PETITE BRIOCHE

1 package dry yeast
⅓ cup sugar, divided
¼ cup warm water (105° to 115°)
½ cup milk
¾ cup butter or margarine, softened
½ teaspoon salt
6 egg yolks
3½ cups all-purpose flour

Dissolve yeast and 1 tablespoon sugar in warm water; stir well, and let stand 5 minutes or until bubbly.

Scald milk; add butter, remaining sugar, and salt. Stir until butter melts. Let mixture cool to lukewarm (105° to 115°). Combine yeast mixture, milk mixture, egg yolks, and flour in a large mixing bowl, and beat at medium speed of an electric mixer 8 to 10 minutes or until smooth.

Cover dough and let rise in a warm place (85°), free from drafts, 2 hours or until more than doubled in bulk. Stir dough down; cover and refrigerate overnight.

Set aside one-fourth of dough. Shape remaining dough into 1-inch balls; place balls in lightly greased miniature brioche molds. Shape reserved dough into ⅜-inch balls, rolling one end of each ball to form a tapered, teardrop shape.

Using a floured finger, press down into center of dough in each brioche mold, touching bottom of each mold. Enlarge cavity to shape of tapered end of reserved dough balls. Place tapered end of dough into cavity, rounding upper portion of teardrop to form a smooth ball. Cover and repeat rising procedure 30 minutes or until doubled in bulk.

Bake at 375° for 10 minutes or until golden brown. Yield: about 3 dozen.

DRESSED CUCUMBERS WITH TOMATOES

8 medium cucumbers
½ cup sugar
1 cup vinegar
¼ cup vegetable oil
¼ cup water
8 small tomatoes, cut into wedges

Place cucumbers in ice water to cover in a large mixing bowl; let stand 1 hour. Drain and cut into thin slices. Place in a large mixing bowl, and set aside.

Combine sugar, vinegar, oil, and water in a small mixing bowl, mixing well; pour over reserved cucumbers. Cover and refrigerate overnight.

To serve, arrange drained cucumber slices and tomato wedges on a large serving platter or individual dishes. Yield: 12 to 15 servings.

BRUSSELS SPROUTS

5 pounds fresh brussels sprouts, cleaned
½ cup butter or margarine, melted
2 teaspoons lemon-pepper seasoning

Place brussels sprouts with salt water to barely cover in a large Dutch oven. Bring to a boil. Reduce heat; simmer, uncovered, 20 minutes or until tender. Drain; place in a serving dish, and keep warm.

Combine butter and lemon-pepper seasoning. Pour over brussels sprouts; toss gently. Serve immediately. Yield: 12 to 15 servings.

MRS. HOWARD'S TRIFLE

1 cup sugar
½ cup water
6 eggs, separated
½ teaspoon vanilla
¼ teaspoon salt
1 cup sifted all-purpose flour
1 cup Madeira, divided
Boiled Custard
3 cups whipping cream
½ cup plus 1 tablespoon
   sugar
Fresh strawberries (optional)

Combine 1 cup sugar and water in a small saucepan. Cook over medium heat, stirring frequently, until mixture comes to a boil and sugar dissolves. Continue cooking, stirring frequently, until mixture reaches thread stage (230°). Remove from heat, and set aside.

Beat egg whites (at room temperature) until stiff peaks form. While beating at medium speed of an electric mixer, pour hot syrup in a thin stream over egg whites. Turn mixer to high speed, and continue beating 5 minutes or until mixture cools.

Combine egg yolks, vanilla, and salt; beat until light and lemon colored. Add to egg white mixture; beat well. Sprinkle flour over egg white mixture, ¼ cup at a time, folding well after each addition.

Pour batter into an ungreased 10-inch tube pan. Bake at 325° for 50 minutes or until cake springs back when lightly touched. Remove from oven, and invert pan. Cool 40 minutes; remove from pan, and cool completely on a wire rack.

Beat whipping cream until foamy; gradually add ½ cup plus 1 tablespoon sugar, beating until soft peaks form. Set aside.

Slice cake into ½-inch slices. Line bottom of a 16-cup trifle bowl with one-third of cake slices; sprinkle with ⅓ cup Madeira. Spoon 2 cups chilled Boiled Custard over cake slices; spread one-third of reserved whipped cream over custard. Repeat layering procedure 2 more times, using remaining cake slices, Madeira, Boiled Custard, and whipped cream. Cover and refrigerate overnight.

Garnish with fresh strawberries, if desired. Spoon into individual serving bowls, and serve immediately. Yield: 12 to 15 servings.

Boiled Custard:

1 quart milk, scalded
4 eggs
1 cup sugar
¼ teaspoon salt
1 teaspoon vanilla extract

Scald milk in top of a double boiler over boiling water.

Combine eggs, sugar, and salt in a small mixing bowl, beating well. Gradually stir 1 cup scalded milk into egg mixture; add to remaining hot milk, stirring constantly.

Cook over boiling water, stirring constantly with a metal spoon, until mixture thickens and coats the spoon. Remove from heat; stir in vanilla. Cool to room temperature; chill. Yield: about 1 quart.

Parkhurst in Harwood, Maryland, was the setting of an elegant soiree in 1857.

ORANGE ICE

Grated rind of 3 oranges
2 cups sugar
1 quart water
2 cups freshly squeezed
  orange juice
2 tablespoons freshly
  squeezed lemon juice

Combine rind, sugar, and water in a large non-metallic saucepan, mixing well; bring to a boil. Reduce heat, and simmer, uncovered, 5 minutes. Remove from heat. Strain, discarding rind; cool.

Add orange juice and lemon juice; mix well. Pour mixture into freezer can of a 2-quart hand-turned or electric freezer. Freeze according to manufacturer's instructions. Let ripen 1½ hours. Scoop into bowls, and serve. Yield: 2 quarts.

CHERRY BOUNCE

6 cups fresh cherry halves
1 quart light rum
1 quart water
4 cups sugar

Place cherry halves in a large jar; pour rum over cherries. Cover and refrigerate 2 to 3 weeks.

Drain; reserve rum in a jar in refrigerator. Return cherries to jar; pour water over cherries. Cover and refrigerate 2 to 3 additional weeks.

Drain, reserving water; discard cherries. Combine reserved rum and water in a jar; add sugar; stir well. (More or less sugar may be used, as desired.)

Serve over crushed ice or as a liqueur. Yield: about 1 gallon.

Note: Cherry Bounce may be stored in refrigerator.

An 1890 trade card romanticizing cherry picking.

CLARET CUP

1¾ quarts claret or other dry
  red wine
1 cup sugar
½ cup Cointreau or other
  orange-flavored liqueur
½ cup port wine
Juice of 2 lemons
2 (33.8-ounce) bottles club
  soda, chilled
2 pints fresh strawberries,
  washed, hulled, and halved
Ice cubes

Combine first 5 ingredients in a 2-quart container, stirring well. Chill thoroughly. Just before serving, pour chilled mixture into a punch bowl; stir in club soda, strawberries, and ice cubes. Ladle into individual serving cups. Yield: 1 gallon.

QUEEN'S PUNCH

2 cups strong hot tea
2 cups sugar
2 cups orange juice
1 cup lemon juice
1 cup brandy
1 cup light rum
Ice Ring
2 (750 ml) bottles champagne,
  chilled

Combine tea and sugar in a large pitcher, stirring until sugar dissolves; cool. Add orange juice, lemon juice, brandy, and rum; stir well. Chill.

Pour tea mixture over ice ring in a punch bowl just before serving. Slowly add champagne. Serve immediately. Yield: about 1 gallon.

Ice Ring:

2 cups orange juice
2 cups club soda
Orange slices, seeded
Fresh mint sprigs

Combine orange juice and club soda; stir.

Arrange orange slices and mint in a 4-cup ring mold; gently pour ½ cup orange juice mixture into mold. Freeze. Pour remaining orange juice mixture into frozen mold; freeze until ready to use. Yield: 1 ice ring.

The President's House, reconstructed after the fire of 1814, is depicted in this 1825 sketch.

DOLLEY MADISON'S DRAWING ROOM

Tall, queenly, Quaker-born Dolley Madison was the leavening to staid President Madison's administration. She, who once had to wear her trinkets sewn into a bag under clothes, went the whole route to modish, even outrageous style; her dress and her parties amazed everyone. She had served President Jefferson as hostess and knew the White House inside out. Her first "Drawing Room" was three months in the planning, but Wednesdays from then on saw the Drawing Room she originated become the model for grand-scale entertainment. Dolley's superb "presence" has rarely, if ever, been surpassed. This menu requires a profligate hand.

CHICKEN CROQUETTES
COLD EYE OF ROUND ROAST
STUFFED YELLOW SQUASH
GREEN BEANS WITH NEW POTATOES
OLD SOUTH BEATEN BISCUITS
TINY YEAST ROLLS
GINGER POUND CAKE
LITTLE SEED CAKES
PEACH ICE CREAM
ALMONDS, RAISINS, NUTS, PECANS
TEA
or
COFFEE
ASSORTMENT OF WINES

Serves 24

CHICKEN CROQUETTES

2 (3-pound) broiler-fryers,
  cut up
1 tablespoon salt
½ teaspoon pepper
1 large onion, chopped
3 stalks celery, chopped
1 tablespoon butter or
  margarine
1 cup milk
4 eggs, divided
1 (12-ounce) container
  Standard oysters, drained
  and coarsely chopped
1 teaspoon salt
½ teaspoon pepper
Dash of ground mace
1½ cups cracker crumbs
Vegetable oil

Combine chicken, 1 table-spoon salt, ½ teaspoon pepper, and water to cover in a large Dutch oven. Bring to a boil. Reduce heat; cover and simmer 1 hour or until chicken is tender. Remove chicken from broth; reserve broth for use in other recipes. Cool chicken; remove meat from bones. Grind chicken. Set aside.

Sauté onion and celery in butter in a large skillet until tender. Combine milk and 2 eggs, beating well. Add to sautéed vegetable mixture; cook over low heat, stirring constantly, until thickened and bubbly.

Combine ground chicken, sauce, oysters, 1 teaspoon salt, ½ teaspoon pepper, and mace in a large mixing bowl. Shape mixture into 24 croquettes. Refrigerate at least 1 hour.

Beat remaining 2 eggs in a small bowl. Dip croquettes in egg; roll in cracker crumbs. Cook croquettes in deep hot oil (350°) until golden brown. Drain on paper towels. Serve hot. Yield: 2 dozen.

The Madison's china (server pictured here), thought to have been used after White House china was lost in the War of 1812.

COLD EYE OF ROUND ROAST

1 (5- to 6-pound) eye of round
  roast
1 tablespoon seasoned salt
1 teaspoon pepper
2 cloves garlic, minced
2 tablespoons butter or
  margarine
Horseradish Sauce

Rub roast with seasoned salt, pepper, and garlic. Cover and refrigerate overnight.

Remove from refrigerator; let stand 1 hour. Brown roast on all sides in butter in a large skillet. Place roast on rack in a shallow roasting pan; insert meat thermometer, if desired.

Bake, uncovered, at 300° until desired degree of doneness: about 1 hour and 45 minutes or 140° (rare), about 2 hours or 160° (medium). Cool completely; slice very thin. Serve with Horseradish Sauce. Yield: 24 servings.

Horseradish Sauce:

1 (8-ounce) carton
  commercial sour cream
2 tablespoons prepared
  horseradish
½ teaspoon salt

Combine all ingredients in a small mixing bowl; mix well. Chill. Yield: about 1 cup.

STUFFED YELLOW SQUASH

12 large yellow squash,
  cleaned
1 cup soft breadcrumbs,
  divided
½ cup grated Parmesan
  cheese, divided
¼ cup butter or margarine,
  melted
2 eggs, beaten
3 tablespoons minced onion
3 tablespoons minced fresh
  parsley
1 teaspoon salt

Place whole squash in a large Dutch oven with boiling salted water to cover. Cover and cook 10 minutes or until squash is tender. Drain well, and cool.

Cut each squash in half lengthwise; remove pulp to a large mixing bowl, leaving firm shells. Arrange shells in three lightly greased 13- x 9- x 2-inch baking dishes; set aside.

Add ¾ cup breadcrumbs and ¼ cup Parmesan cheese to squash pulp, mixing well. Stir in melted butter, eggs, onion, parsley, and salt.

Combine remaining breadcrumbs and cheese in a small mixing bowl; set aside.

Spoon 1 heaping tablespoon reserved squash mixture into each prepared shell. Sprinkle each with reserved breadcrumb mixture. Bake, uncovered, at 400° for 25 minutes or until breadcrumb mixture is lightly browned. Serve immediately. Yield: 24 servings.

GREEN BEANS WITH NEW POTATOES

⅓ pound salt pork, cut into
  ½-inch cubes
1 gallon water
6 pounds fresh green beans,
  snapped
1 large onion, coarsely
  chopped
1 teaspoon salt
1 teaspoon pepper
24 new potatoes,
  cleaned

Place salt pork and water in a large stockpot; cover and cook over medium heat 1 hour. Add green beans, onion, salt, and pepper; cover and simmer 30 minutes.

Pare a 1-inch strip around center of each potato; add to green beans. Cover and simmer 50 minutes or until vegetables are tender. Transfer to a serving dish. Yield: 24 servings.

OLD SOUTH BEATEN BISCUITS

4 cups all-purpose
  flour
Dash of baking soda
1 teaspoon salt
¼ cup plus 1 tablespoon
  shortening
½ cup milk, chilled
½ cup ice water

Sift together flour, soda, and salt in a large mixing bowl; stir well. Cut in shortening with a pastry blender until mixture resembles coarse meal. Sprinkle milk and water evenly over flour mixture, stirring until dry ingredients are moistened.

Turn dough out onto a lightly floured surface. Beat with a rolling pin or wooden mallet for 30 minutes or until blisters appear, folding dough over frequently. Roll to ¼-inch thickness; cut with a 1¾-inch biscuit cutter. Prick each biscuit with the tines of a fork. Place on lightly greased baking sheets. Bake at 350° for 45 minutes or until lightly browned. Yield: about 4 dozen.

TINY YEAST ROLLS

1 package dry yeast
½ cup warm water (105° to
  115°)
1 cup boiling water
¾ cup shortening
2 teaspoons salt
½ cup sugar
1 egg, beaten
5½ cups all-purpose flour

Dissolve yeast in warm water, stirring well. Let stand 5 minutes or until bubbly.

Combine boiling water, shortening, salt, and sugar in a large mixing bowl; stir. Cool mixture to lukewarm (105° to 115°). Stir in beaten egg, dissolved yeast, and flour.

Cover and let rise in a warm place (85°), free from drafts, 1 hour or until doubled in bulk. Shape dough into a ball; place in a greased bowl, turning to grease top. Cover and refrigerate at least 4 hours or overnight.

Shape dough into 1½-inch balls; place balls in 1¾-inch muffin pans. Cover and repeat rising procedure 30 minutes or until doubled in bulk. Bake at 450° for 6 minutes or until golden brown. Yield: 6½ dozen.

Dolley Payne Todd Madison, by Bass Otis, c.1817.

GINGER POUND CAKE

2 cups butter or margarine,
  softened
2⅓ cups firmly packed
  brown sugar
6 eggs
½ cup molasses
3 cups all-purpose flour
2 teaspoons baking powder
1 tablespoon ground ginger
1 tablespoon ground
  allspice
1 tablespoon ground
  cinnamon
Grated rind of 2 lemons
1 tablespoon lemon
  juice
4 (10-inch) strips lemon
  rind (optional)
Lemon slices (optional)

Cream butter in a large mixing bowl; gradually add sugar, beating until light and fluffy. Add eggs, one at a time, beating well after each addition. Add molasses, mixing well.

Combine flour, baking powder, ginger, allspice, and cinnamon in a medium mixing bowl; mix well. Gradually add to creamed mixture, mixing well after each addition. Stir in lemon rind and juice.

Pour batter into a well-greased 10-inch tube pan. Bake at 325° for 1 hour and 25 minutes or until cake springs back when lightly touched. Cool in pan 10 to 15 minutes; remove cake from pan, and cool completely on a wire rack.

Tie each lemon strip into a bow; place on top of cake, and arrange lemon slices around base of cake, if desired. Yield: one 10-inch cake.

Peach Ice Cream is good with Little Seed Cakes and Ginger Pound Cake.

LITTLE SEED CAKES

¼ cup plus 2 tablespoons
  butter or margarine,
  softened
1 cup firmly packed brown
  sugar
1 egg, lightly beaten
½ cup all-purpose flour
¼ teaspoon baking powder
Dash of salt
½ teaspoon vanilla extract
¼ cup plus 2 tablespoons
  sesame seeds, lightly
  toasted

Cream butter in a large mixing bowl; gradually add sugar, beating well. Add egg; mix well. Combine flour, baking powder, and salt; add to creamed mixture, stirring well. Stir in vanilla and sesame seeds.

Drop dough by teaspoonfuls 2 inches apart onto lightly greased cookie sheets. Bake at 375° for 4 to 5 minutes. Cool slightly on cookie sheets; remove to wire racks to cool completely. Yield: about 5 dozen.

PEACH ICE CREAM

2 cups sliced fresh peaches
½ cup sugar
9 egg yolks, lightly beaten
1 cup plus 2 tablespoons
  sugar
⅛ teaspoon salt
3 cups milk, scalded
2¼ teaspoons vanilla extract
3 cups whipping cream,
  whipped

Combine peaches and ½ cup sugar; stir well. Mash peaches, and set aside.

Combine egg, sugar, and salt in top of a double boiler; stir in milk. Cook over simmering water, stirring constantly, until mixture thickens and coats a metal spoon. Remove from heat, and cool. Stir in reserved peaches and vanilla. Fold in whipped cream.

Pour mixture into freezer can of a 5-quart hand-turned or electric freezer. Freeze according to manufacturer's instructions. Let ripen 1½ to 2 hours before serving. Scoop ice cream into individual serving bowls, and serve immediately. Yield: about 5 quarts.

SATURDAY NIGHT GERMANS IN SAVANNAH

Dear Miss J——: If you have no engagement for the 7th. German, I will be very glad if you will let me have the pleasure of escorting you. Very sincerely, S.E., Jr." In the late 1880s, Savannah youths were in the midst of a delightful informal kind of party craze: the german, which became the most popular of entertainments. The parties were held every two weeks by the male socialite members of the exclusive German Club. The same people attended each time; it was almost like a family of 100 to 150 dancers. The germans were held in the old Armory Hall ballroom, where, after a late night supper, they danced to the music of Natty Solomon and his band. Protocol had been established beforehand: "breaks" were permissible.

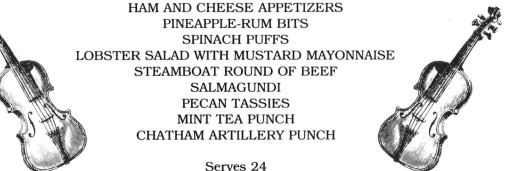

HAM AND CHEESE APPETIZERS
PINEAPPLE-RUM BITS
SPINACH PUFFS
LOBSTER SALAD WITH MUSTARD MAYONNAISE
STEAMBOAT ROUND OF BEEF
SALMAGUNDI
PECAN TASSIES
MINT TEA PUNCH
CHATHAM ARTILLERY PUNCH

Serves 24

Dancing at the DeSoto Hotel in Savannah, Georgia, 1946.

HAM AND CHEESE APPETIZERS

1 (3-ounce) package cream
  cheese, softened
2 tablespoons mayonnaise
1 tablespoon olive liquid
½ teaspoon prepared mustard
2 tablespoons chopped onion
⅔ cup chopped, cooked ham
16 slices thin-sliced whole
  wheat bread, crust removed
Pimiento-stuffed olive slices

Combine cream cheese, mayonnaise, olive liquid, mustard, and onion in container of an electric blender; process until smooth. Add ham, and process just until blended. Set aside.

Cut bread with assorted 2-inch cookie cutters; toast lightly on each side. Spread each with 1 teaspoon reserved ham mixture. Garnish each with an olive slice. Yield: about 4 dozen.

PINEAPPLE-RUM BITS

1 (20-ounce) can pineapple
  chunks, undrained
1 cup light rum
½ cup sugar

Combine pineapple, rum, and sugar in a glass or plastic container, mixing well. Cover and refrigerate 1 week.

Drain well; discard rum mixture, and serve in individual compotes. Yield: 24 servings.

Note: Pineapple Chunk Rum Bits may be served in fresh pineapple halves.

SPINACH PUFFS

5 (10-ounce) packages frozen
  chopped spinach, thawed
3 bunches green onions,
  finely chopped
1 small bunch parsley, finely
  chopped
1 pound feta cheese,
  crumbled
½ cup grated Parmesan
  cheese
3 tablespoons vegetable oil
3 tablespoons cream of
  wheat, uncooked
6 eggs, beaten
1 (16-ounce) package frozen
  phyllo pastry, thawed
2 cups butter or margarine,
  melted

Place spinach on paper towels, and squeeze until barely moist. Combine spinach, onion, parsley, cheese, oil, cream of wheat, and beaten eggs in a large mixing bowl; mix well.

Place two sheets phyllo on a dry surface; brush each sheet lightly with melted butter. Layer sheets, butter sides up. Keep remaining sheets covered, according to package directions.

Cut layered phyllo sheets lengthwise into 2-inch strips. Place 1 teaspoon spinach mixture at base of each strip, folding the right bottom corner over it into a triangle. Continue folding back and forth into a triangle to the end of strip. Repeat procedure with remaining phyllo and spinach mixture.

Place triangles, seam side down, on 15- x 10- x 1-inch jellyroll pans. Bake at 325° for 20 to 25 minutes. Yield: about 12 dozen.

Note: Spinach Puffs may be frozen. Place frozen puffs on jellyroll pans; bake as directed.

A fine lobster is served.

LOBSTER SALAD WITH MUSTARD MAYONNAISE

8 cups chopped, cooked
  lobster (about 10 lobster
  tails)
4 cups chopped celery
½ cup finely chopped green
  or red pepper
1½ cups mayonnaise
¼ cup commercial sour
  cream
2 tablespoons Dijon mustard
1 tablespoon plus 1 teaspoon
  lemon juice
1 teaspoon salt
¼ teaspoon pepper
Shredded lettuce
Fresh watercress
Hard-cooked eggs, cut into
  wedges
Steamed asparagus tips,
  chilled

Combine lobster, celery, and chopped pepper in a large mixing bowl; toss lightly. Combine mayonnaise, sour cream, mustard, lemon juice, salt, and pepper; stir well. Add to lobster mixture; toss well. Cover and chill thoroughly.

Arrange lettuce on a serving platter. Place lobster salad in center; arrange watercress, egg wedges, and asparagus around salad. Yield: 24 servings.

STEAMBOAT ROUND OF BEEF

1 (16½-pound) beef round
Vegetable oil
Fresh parsley sprigs

Tie roast securely with heavy cord. Brush entire surface with oil, and place in a shallow roasting pan. Add water to a depth of 1 inch. Insert meat thermometer in meaty part of roast, being careful not to touch fat or bone.

Bake, uncovered, at 350° for 2 hours. Reduce heat to 275°, and continue to bake, uncovered, until meat thermometer registers desired degree of doneness: about 1½ hours or 140° (rare), about 2½ hours or 160° (medium), about 3 hours or 170° (well done). If roast gets too brown, cover lightly with aluminum foil.

Remove cord, and transfer roast to a serving platter. Garnish with fresh parsley. Let stand 15 minutes before carving. Yield: 24 servings.

SALMAGUNDI

1 head leaf lettuce, torn
1 head red leaf lettuce, torn
1 small head purple cabbage, chopped
1 bunch celery, chopped
3 large cucumbers, peeled and thinly sliced
1 (12-ounce) jar sweet whole gherkin pickles, drained
2 (6-ounce) jars marinated artichoke hearts, drained and coarsely chopped
1 bunch fresh scallions, chopped
1 bunch fresh watercress, chopped
1 small bunch fresh parsley, chopped
1 large purple onion, sliced
Mary Randolph's Salad Dressing

Arrange all ingredients, except Mary Randolph's Salad Dressing, attractively on a serving platter. Serve with Mary Randolph's Salad Dressing. Yield: 24 servings.

Mary Randolph's Salad Dressing:

12 hard-cooked eggs, cut in half
¼ cup plus 2 tablespoons water
¾ cup soybean oil
¼ cup plus 2 tablespoons cider vinegar
¼ cup plus 2 tablespoons tarragon vinegar
1½ tablespoons prepared mustard
¼ cup plus 2 tablespoons sugar
1½ teaspoons salt
1 small bunch green onions with tops, finely chopped

Place egg yolks in a medium mixing bowl; slice whites, and reserve for salad garnish. Add water to yolks, and mash until smooth. Add remaining ingredients; stir until well blended. Chill thoroughly. Yield: about 1 quart.

Salmagundi, a favorite salad of Dolley Madison's.

The Georgia Chatham Artillery Company at Jackson's Tomb.

MINT TEA PUNCH

1 gallon boiling water
4 cups fresh mint leaves
1 cup tea leaves
4 cups sugar
2 (46-ounce) cans pineapple
  juice, chilled
2 cups lemon juice, chilled
Fresh mint sprigs

Pour boiling water over mint leaves and tea leaves in a large container; cover and let steep 30 minutes. Strain, discarding leaves. Add sugar, stirring well; chill.

Add pineapple juice and lemon juice just before serving, stirring well. Pour over ice, and garnish each serving with a fresh mint sprig. Yield: about 2 gallons.

CHATHAM ARTILLERY PUNCH

1 (4-ounce) can green tea
2 quarts cold water
Juice of 9 oranges
Juice of 9 lemons
1 (1-pound) package light
  brown sugar
½ cup firmly packed light
  brown sugar
2 (10-ounce) jars maraschino
  cherries, drained
3 liters Rhine wine
1 liter white Virgin Island rum
1 liter brandy
1 liter gin
1 (750-milliliter) bottle Rye
  whiskey
3 (750-milliliter) bottles
  champagne, chilled

Combine tea and water. Let stand overnight; press and strain, discarding leaves. Combine tea and remaining ingredients, except champagne, in a non-metal 5-gallon container; stir well. Cover and let ferment 4 weeks in a cool, dark place.

Strain liquid; discard cherries. Pour liquid into bottles. Chill as needed. Just before serving, dilute each gallon of chilled stock with 1 bottle of champagne, and pour over an ice mold in a punch bowl. Yield: about 3 gallons.

PECAN TASSIES

⅓ cup sugar
⅓ cup firmly packed brown
  sugar
1 egg
2 teaspoons butter or
  margarine, melted
Dash of salt
¼ teaspoon vanilla extract
½ cup finely chopped pecans
Cream Cheese Pastry
Powdered sugar (optional)

Combine sugar and egg in a small mixing bowl; beat well. Add melted butter, salt, vanilla, and pecans, mixing well.

Spoon 1 teaspoon pecan mixture into each Cream Cheese Pastry shell. Bake at 350° for 20 minutes or until pastry is lightly browned. Cool slightly in muffin pans. Remove to wire racks, and cool completely. Sift powdered sugar lightly over tarts, if desired. Yield: 4 dozen.

Cream Cheese Pastry:

2 (3-ounce) packages cream
  cheese, softened
1 cup butter, softened
2 cups all-purpose
  flour

Combine all ingredients; mix well. Shape into a ball, and chill 15 minutes. Divide dough into forty-eight 1-inch balls, and place in ungreased 1¾-inch muffin pans. Shape each into a shell. Yield: pastry for 4 dozen miniature tarts.

ANNAPOLIS RING DANCE BANQUET

The Ring Dance Banquet at the U.S. Naval Academy is a tradition that goes back to 1925. Before that time, a second classman could put on his class ring as soon as he passed his navigation finals. First classmen seized the moment to dump rings and wearers into Dewey Basin to "baptize" them. For the Ring Dance, the men's dates (called drags) wear the class rings on ribbons around their necks until after a sumptuous banquet. Then, in a touchingly choreographed ceremony in the ballroom, the girls christen the rings in a binnacle of water the Navy has supplied from the Seven Seas and slip them on the proud midshipmen's fingers.

MARINATED SHRIMP COCKTAIL
ENDIVE SALAD WITH STILTON DRESSING
BEEF WELLINGTON
SPINACH STUFFED TOMATOES
CHOCOLATE DIPPED STRAWBERRIES

Serves 10 to 12

Midshipman and "drag" arrive at 1939 Ring Dance through ring replica.

*Marinated Shrimp
Cocktail to tempt the
saints. Begin with
seasoned butter.*

MARINATED SHRIMP COCKTAIL

¾ cup butter or margarine, melted
1½ teaspoons Old Bay seasoning
¾ teaspoon paprika
3 pounds medium shrimp
1⅓ cups olive oil
1⅓ cups vinegar
¼ cup capers
1½ tablespoons Italian herb seasoning
1 clove garlic, minced
12 thin lemon slices
Fresh parsley sprigs

Combine butter, Old Bay seasoning, and paprika in a large skillet; stir well. Add shrimp; cook over medium heat, stirring constantly, 5 minutes or until shrimp are done. Drain; rinse with cold water. Peel and devein shrimp; place in a 13- x 9- x 2-inch baking dish. Set aside.

Place olive oil in a medium mixing bowl; gradually add vinegar, beating constantly with a wire whisk. Stir in capers, Italian herb seasoning, and garlic; pour over shrimp. Cover and refrigerate overnight.

Place shrimp in a serving bowl on ice; discard marinade. Garnish with lemon and parsley. Yield: 10 to 12 servings.

ENDIVE SALAD WITH STILTON DRESSING

1 head endive, torn
1 head Boston bibb lettuce, torn
2 (12-ounce) cans artichoke hearts, drained
1 large red onion, thinly sliced and separated into rings
Stilton Dressing

Combine endive, lettuce, artichoke hearts, and onion in a large serving bowl; toss lightly. Serve with Stilton Dressing. Yield: 10 to 12 servings.

Stilton Dressing:

½ cup firmly packed brown sugar
½ cup red wine vinegar
1 cup peanut oil
½ cup catsup
1 tablespoon lemon juice
2 teaspoons onion juice
½ teaspoon garlic powder
½ teaspoon salt
¼ teaspoon white pepper
¼ teaspoon dry mustard
5 ounces Stilton cheese, crumbled

Combine sugar and vinegar in a medium mixing bowl, mixing well. Add oil, catsup, lemon juice, onion juice, garlic powder, salt, pepper, and dry mustard, stirring well; add cheese, stirring well. Cover and refrigerate at least 3 hours. Yield: about 3 cups.

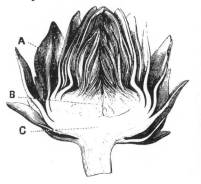

BEEF WELLINGTON

1 (4- to 5-pound) beef tenderloin, trimmed
1½ teaspoons salt
½ teaspoon pepper
½ pound fresh mushrooms, chopped
2 tablespoons chopped shallots
2 ounces chopped, cooked ham
¼ cup Madeira
3 tablespoons butter or margarine
1 (4-ounce) can liver pâté
1 (14-ounce) package frozen puff pastry, thawed
1 egg, beaten
Watercress

Sprinkle roast with salt and pepper. Place on a rack in a shallow roasting pan, tucking narrow end under to make roast more uniformly thick. Bake, uncovered, at 450° for 35 minutes. Cool to room temperature.

Combine mushrooms, shallots, ham, Madeira, and butter in a medium skillet; cook over medium heat, stirring frequently, until all liquid is absorbed. Set aside.

Spread pâté evenly over cooled tenderloin; spread reserved mushroom mixture over pâté.

Roll thawed pastry on a lighty floured surface into a rectangle, 1½ inches larger in width and length than roast. Place roast, top side down, in center of pastry. Bring sides of pastry up to overlap on underside of roast, forming a seam; trim, reserving excess pastry. Fold over ends of pastry to seal. Invert tenderloin onto an ungreased 15- x 10- x 1-inch jellyroll pan.

Brush pastry with beaten egg. Roll pastry trimmings to ⅛-inch thickness on a lightly floured surface; cut into decorative shapes, and arrange on surface of pastry, as desired. Brush shapes with beaten egg. Bake, uncovered, at 425° for 30 minutes or until pastry is lightly browned. Let stand 10 minutes. Place on a warm serving platter garnished with watercress, and carve into ¾-inch slices. Yield: 10 to 12 servings.

SPINACH STUFFED TOMATOES

6 medium-size ripe, firm
   tomatoes
1 medium onion, chopped
1 clove garlic, minced
2 tablespoons butter or
   margarine
3 (10-ounce) packages frozen
   chopped spinach, thawed
   and drained
1 (16-ounce) carton
   commercial sour cream
2 tablespoons Worcestershire
   sauce
1½ teaspoons salt
½ teaspoon pepper
¼ cup buttered breadcrumbs

Cut tomatoes in half crosswise; scoop out pulp, leaving
shells intact (reserve pulp for
other uses). Invert tomato shells
on paper towels to drain.

Sauté onion and garlic in butter in a large skillet until tender.
Add spinach, sour cream, Worcestershire sauce, salt, and pepper, mixing well. Cook over
medium heat, stirring constantly, 3 minutes or until thoroughly heated.

Fill tomato shells with spinach mixture; sprinkle with
breadcrumbs. Place stuffed tomatoes in a 13- x 9- x 2-inch
baking dish. Bake, uncovered,
at 350° for 15 to 20 minutes.
Yield: 10 to 12 servings.

CHOCOLATE DIPPED STRAWBERRIES

3 pints medium strawberries
¾ pound chocolate,
   processed for dipping

Wash strawberries, leaving
stems intact. Drain well.

Place chocolate in a medium-
size stoneware bowl, and set
bowl in a pan of boiling water.
Stir constantly with a wooden
spoon just until chocolate
melts. (Too much heat will affect
dipping quality of chocolate.)

Dip each strawberry halfway
into chocolate; place on a baking sheet; refrigerate. Arrange
chilled berries in a serving bowl.
Yield: 10 to 12 servings.

A scene from the Naval Academy Ball of 1869.

GEORGE WASHINGTON'S BIRTH NIGHT CELEBRATION

On February 11, 1799, George Washington's Birth Night was observed when the population of Alexandria, Virginia, lined the streets to see their hero ride into town accompanied by three companies of dragoons. For his entertainment, a mock battle was staged, and that evening he and Mrs. Washington attended a ball which was " . . . much superior to anything ever known here. . . . The company was numerous. . . . " Formal dances followed an elegant supper. Celebrations of Washington's Birth Night did not stop with his death later that year. An 1805 Birth Night Ball featured "costly viands" and an imposing statue of the revered general.

BAKED VIRGINIA HAM MADEIRA
ROAST TENDERLOIN OF BEEF WITH BÉARNAISE SAUCE
DEVILED OYSTERS
SALLY LUNN
SNOWY NESTS WITH PINEAPPLE AND SPUN SUGAR

Serves 16

BAKED VIRGINIA HAM MADEIRA

1 (12- to 13-pound) country ham
1 cup Madeira
1 small onion, finely chopped
2 tablespoons butter or margarine
2 tablespoons all-purpose flour
2 cups rich beef stock or bouillon
2 tablespoons tomato paste

Place ham in a large container; cover with cold water, and soak overnight. Remove ham from water, and drain. Scrub ham thoroughly with a stiff brush, and rinse with cold water.

Replace ham in container, and cover with fresh cold water. Bring to a boil. Reduce heat; cover and simmer 4 hours. Remove ham from water; discard water. Remove skin, and trim fat to a thin layer. Score fat in a diamond pattern.

Place ham, fat side up, in a shallow roasting pan. Pour Madeira over ham. Cover with a lid or aluminum foil. Bake at 350° for 30 minutes.

Sauté onion in butter in a large skillet until tender. Add flour; cook over medium heat 2 to 3 minutes, stirring constantly. Gradually add beef stock; cook, stirring constantly, until thickened and bubbly. Stir in tomato paste; cook over medium heat, stirring often, 10 minutes or until mixture is reduced by half.

Spoon sauce over ham in roasting pan. Bake, uncovered, at 350° for 30 minutes or until browned. Transfer to a serving platter; cut ham diagonally into thin slices. Yield: 16 servings.

This painting by Daniel Huntington, 1861, depicts the regal elegance of George Washington and his "Republican court."

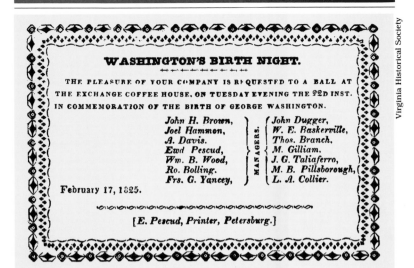

WASHINGTON'S BIRTH NIGHT.

THE PLEASURE OF YOUR COMPANY IS REQUESTED TO A BALL AT THE EXCHANGE COFFEE HOUSE, ON TUESDAY EVENING THE 22D INST. IN COMMEMORATION OF THE BIRTH OF GEORGE WASHINGTON.

MANAGERS.
John H. Brown,
Joel Hammon,
A. Davis.
Ewd Pescud,
Wm. B. Wood,
Ro. Bolling.
Frs. G. Yancey,

John Dugger,
W. E. Baskerville,
Thos. Branch.
M. Gilliam.
J. G. Taliaferro,
M. B. Pillsborough,
L. A. Collier.

February 17, 1825.

[E. Pescud, Printer, Petersburg.]

An invitation to Washington's Birth Night Ball, which was patterned after the King's Birth Night celebration, was sent by fourteen Virginians. A similar ball in 1848 was given by Mrs. Polk, Mrs. Madison, Mrs. Adams, and Mrs. Hamilton — wives of prominent statesmen.

ROAST TENDERLOIN OF BEEF WITH BÉARNAISE SAUCE

1 (6- to 7-pound) beef tenderloin, trimmed
¼ cup butter, softened
1 (10½-ounce) can beef consommé, undiluted
3 (14-ounce) cans artichoke hearts, drained and steamed
2 pounds small mushrooms, steamed
3 (12-ounce) packages baby carrots, scraped and steamed
Béarnaise Sauce

Béarnaise Sauce:

1½ cups vermouth
2 tablespoons vinegar
2 green onions, chopped
½ cup chopped fresh parsley
2 teaspoons dried tarragon leaves
⅛ teaspoon dried chervil leaves
4 whole peppercorns
2 cups butter, melted
6 egg yolks
⅛ teaspoon dried tarragon leaves

Rub tenderloin with butter; place on a rack in a shallow roasting pan. Insert meat thermometer. Baste with consommé. Bake, uncovered, at 350° for 1 hour or until meat thermometer registers 140° (rare); baste often.

Remove tenderloin to a warm, large platter. Surround with warm artichoke hearts, mushrooms, and carrots. Place on a warm serving platter. Serve immediately with Béarnaise Sauce. Yield: 16 servings.

Combine first 7 ingredients in a small saucepan. Bring to a boil; boil 5 minutes or until mixture is reduced by half. Strain; discard spices, and cool.

Combine melted butter and egg yolks, beating well. Gradually add to cooled vermouth mixture, stirring constantly. Cook over low heat, stirring constantly, until thickened. Stir in ⅛ teaspoon tarragon. Serve immediately. Yield: about 3 cups.

DEVILED OYSTERS

6 (12-ounce) containers
  Standard oysters, drained
2 cups whipping cream
¾ cup cracker crumbs
¼ cup butter or margarine,
  divided
½ teaspoon salt
¼ teaspoon pepper
⅛ teaspoon red pepper
¾ cup soft breadcrumbs

Cut oysters in half; place oysters, whipping cream, cracker crumbs, 1 tablespoon butter, salt, and pepper in a medium saucepan. Cook over medium heat, stirring constantly, 10 minutes or until thoroughly heated.

Pour mixture into a 13- x 9- x 2-inch baking dish. Sprinkle with breadcrumbs; dot with remaining butter. Bake at 350° for 30 minutes. Remove from oven; let stand 20 minutes before serving. Yield: 16 servings.

SALLY LUNN

1 package dry yeast
¼ cup warm water (105° to
  115°)
¾ cup warm milk (105° to
  115°)
½ cup butter or margarine,
  softened
⅓ cup sugar
3 eggs, well beaten
4 cups all-purpose flour
1 teaspoon salt

Combine yeast and water; let stand 5 minutes. Stir in milk.

Cream butter; gradually add sugar, beating until light and fluffy. Add eggs, mixing well. Combine flour and salt; add to creamed mixture alternately with yeast mixture, beginning and ending with flour mixture. Cover and let rise in a warm place (85°), free from drafts, 1 hour or until doubled in bulk.

Spoon batter into a well-greased 10-inch tube pan. Cover and repeat rising procedure until doubled in bulk. Bake at 350° for 40 to 50 minutes. Remove from pan; cool on a wire rack. Yield: one 10-inch loaf.

SNOWY NESTS
WITH PINEAPPLE AND SPUN SUGAR

4 egg whites
½ teaspoon cream of tartar
¼ teaspoon almond
  extract
¼ teaspoon salt
1½ cups superfine sugar
2 (15¼-ounce) cans pineapple
  tidbits, well drained
Spun Sugar

Beat egg whites (at room temperature), cream of tartar, almond extract, and salt in a large mixing bowl until foamy. Gradually add sugar, 1 tablespoon at a time, beating until stiff peaks form and sugar dissolves. (Do not underbeat mixture.)

Draw 16 circles, 2½ inches in diameter, on a parchment-lined baking sheet. Spoon meringue mixture into circles. Shape meringue into shells, using the back of a spoon. (Sides should be about 1½ inches high.) Bake at 225° for 1 hour. Turn oven off; cool in oven at least 1 hour. (Do not open oven door.) Remove from parchment and use immediately.

Fill meringue shells with well-drained pineapple. Wrap pineapple with Spun Sugar. Serve immediately. Yield: 16 servings.

Spun Sugar:

2 cups sugar
½ cup water
⅛ teaspoon cream of
  tartar

Combine sugar, water, and cream of tartar in a medium saucepan. Cook over medium heat, stirring frequently, until mixture comes to a boil. Continue cooking until mixture reaches hard crack stage (310°). Remove from heat.

Hold 2 dinner forks back to back. Dip forks into syrup, and as syrup runs off, pull forks apart, allowing threads to spin down onto a sheet of waxed paper. Repeat procedure until desired number of threads are spun. (Reheat syrup over low heat, as needed for consistency.) Yield: Spun Sugar for 16 meringue shells.

Colonial costumes, 1910, on Washington's birthday.

---

ast Tenderloin of Beef with garnish, Béarnaise Sauce, and Sally Lunn.

View of the entrance to the Ponce de León Hotel, c.1890.

THE HERMITAGE BALL
AND SUPPER IN ST. AUGUSTINE

The Hermitage Association of Nashville had struggled for over two years on the restoration of General Andrew Jackson's Tennessee home when, in 1892, a benefit was given in St. Augustine, Florida, which gave the project a tremendous push. Jackson had been identified with Florida's early history, and people of power came together to sponsor one of the most brilliant social affairs ever recorded in this country. Pullman cars were available for hundreds of out-of-state guests. Henry Flagler threw open the Ponce de León. The dining room became a ballroom, and the supper, an incredible feast featuring Galantine of Turkey, was served in the side rooms.

GALANTINE OF TURKEY
OLD ST. AUGUSTINE SEAFOOD SALAD
ORANGE-PINEAPPLE AMBROSIA
GÂTEAU AUX AMANDES
or
STRAWBERRY FLAMBÉ
COFFEE
WINE
CHAMPAGNE

Serves 24

GALANTINE OF TURKEY

1 (12- to 13-pound) turkey
½ teaspoon salt
⅜ teaspoon pepper, divided
1 pound finely ground veal
1 pound finely ground ham
¼ teaspoon ground thyme
¼ teaspoon rubbed sage
⅛ teaspoon celery salt
4 mushrooms, sliced
3 hard-cooked egg yolks, sliced
¼ cup pistachio nuts
6 thin strips tongue
1 gallon boiling water
3 stalks celery, cut into 2-inch pieces
2 carrots, scraped and cut into 1-inch pieces
1 small onion, sliced
1 teaspoon whole peppercorns
12 whole cloves
Butter or margarine
Green onion stems
Additional mushroom slices
Hard-cooked egg slices
Pimiento pieces
4 envelopes unflavored gelatin
2½ cups water, divided
2 (10½-ounce) cans consommé

Remove giblets from turkey, and cut off tail and wing tips (reserve for other uses). Rinse turkey with cold water, and pat dry.

Place turkey, breast side down, on a cutting board. Using a small, sharp boning knife, cut down one side of backbone and around pocket of flesh just above the thigh joint, keeping pocket attached to flesh and skin. Cut through thigh ball joint directly below pocket of flesh. Cut through wing ball joint left of shoulder bone.

Cutting close to frame, pull skin and flesh away. (Do not cut or tear skin near breast bone.) Reverse turkey, and repeat boning procedure on other side. Cut through cartilage as necessary to avoid tearing skin; remove frame.

Hold each wing straight up. Cut tendon free; scrape flesh downward to remove bone. Cut along length of each thigh bone to ball joint. Cut and scrape flesh to remove bone. Leave drumstick bone intact.

Spread boned turkey flat. Slice and trim turkey, leaving a uniform layer of flesh over surface of skin. Slice excess flesh into 1-inch-wide strips; set aside.

Sprinkle inside of boned turkey with salt and ½ teaspoon pepper. Combine veal, ham, thyme, sage, celery salt, and remaining pepper, mixing well. Spread evenly over boned turkey. Layer mushrooms, egg yolks, and pistachio nuts on veal mixture. Arrange reserved turkey strips and tongue strips over entire surface.

Sew skin closed, using a darning needle. Begin at tail, sewing toward neck. Fold back excess neck skin under wings; sew wing skin to turkey. Run a skewer through legs to hold shape. Wrap turkey in 5 layers of buttered cheesecloth; pull layers tight to restore form. Tie ends tight, using kitchen string. Tie middle of roll, using a strip of cheesecloth.

Combine boiling water, celery, carrots, onion, peppercorns, and cloves in a large stockpot. Place turkey in boiling water; cover and reduce heat. Simmer 1½ to 2 hours or until roll becomes firm. Remove to a large platter. Remove and discard cheesecloth; cover turkey and chill.

Garnish turkey with green onion strips, mushroom slices, hard-cooked egg slices, and pimiento pieces. Set turkey on a wire rack placed over a large shallow pan.

Soften gelatin in 1 cup water. Combine consommé and remaining water in a medium saucepan; bring to a boil. Remove consommé from heat; add softened gelatin, stirring until gelatin dissolves. Cool to room temperature. Spoon glaze over turkey. Chill to set. Repeat glazing procedure 5 times, chilling at least 5 minutes between applications. Refrigerate until ready to serve. Place galantine on a serving platter. Cut remaining aspic with a fork; spoon around galantine onto platter. Slice and serve. Yield: 24 servings.

Galantine of Turkey with Champagne.

OLD ST. AUGUSTINE SEAFOOD SALAD

1 head iceberg lettuce, shredded
1 pound lump crabmeat
1 cup diced celery
Pimiento strips
2 pounds lobster tails, steamed
Capers
4 pounds medium shrimp, cooked and deveined
Ripe olives
Fresh watercress sprigs
St. Augustine Seafood Sauce
Country Club Salad Dressing

Arrange lettuce on a large oval platter; set aside.

Combine crabmeat and celery, mixing well. Mound crabmeat mixture in center of lettuce on platter; garnish with pimiento strips.

Cut lobster into 1-inch cubes; arrange in a circle around crabmeat, and garnish with capers. Arrange shrimp around lobster; garnish shrimp with ripe olives. Chill thoroughly.

Garnish platter with fresh watercress sprigs. Serve with St. Augustine Seafood Sauce and Country Club Salad Dressing. Yield: 24 servings.

St. Augustine Seafood Sauce:

2 cups mayonnaise
2 tablespoons tarragon vinegar
1 tablespoon prepared mustard
⅓ cup minced sour pickle
3 tablespoons capers
1 tablespoon minced fresh parsley

Combine all ingredients; mix well. Cover and chill thoroughly. Yield: about 2½ cups.

Country Club Salad Dressing:

1 cup mayonnaise
½ cup chili sauce
1 tablespoon prepared mustard
Hot sauce to taste

Combine all ingredients; mix well. Chill thoroughly. Yield: about 1½ cups.

ORANGE-PINEAPPLE AMBROSIA

12 oranges, peeled, sliced, and seeded
3 pineapples, peeled, cored, and sliced
2 cups grated coconut
1 cup sifted powdered sugar
1 cup lime juice
1 tablespoon grenadine
Maraschino cherries

Alternate layers of oranges, pineapple, coconut, and sugar in a large serving bowl. Combine lime juice and grenadine; pour over fruit. Cover and chill thoroughly. Garnish ambrosia with cherries before serving. Yield: 24 servings.

GÂTEAU AUX AMANDES

1 cup water
½ cup butter or margarine
Dash of salt
1 cup all-purpose flour
4 eggs
1½ cups whipping cream
¼ cup sifted powdered sugar
½ gallon cherry ice cream
½ cup toasted sliced almonds

Combine water, butter, and salt in a medium saucepan; bring to a boil. Add flour all at once; cook over medium heat, stirring constantly, until mixture leaves sides of pan and forms a ball. Remove from heat. Add eggs, one at a time, beating vigorously after each addition. Beat until mixture is smooth and shiny.

Drop by tablespoonfuls 3 inches apart onto an ungreased cookie sheet, making 12 individual puffs. Mark an 8-inch circle on another ungreased cookie sheet. Place remaining mixture in a pastry bag fitted with a large, plain tip. Pipe onto cookie sheet, using marked circle as a guide for inside diameter.

Bake puffs and ring at 400°

for 20 minutes or until golden brown; turn oven off. Let cool completely in oven, leaving door slightly ajar.

Beat whipping cream until foamy; gradually add sugar, beating until stiff peaks form.

Cut puffs and ring in half horizontally. Fill lower half of puffs and ring with ice cream; replace tops. Place ring on a large serving plate; place puffs in center of ring. Garnish top of puffs and ring with sweetened whipped cream; sprinkle with toasted almonds. Serve immediately. Yield: 24 servings.

STRAWBERRY FLAMBÉ

1 gallon vanilla ice cream, softened
24 almond macaroons, crumbled
1 cup almonds, toasted and chopped
1 cup Grand Marnier, divided
2 quarts fresh strawberries, washed, hulled, and halved
1 cup sugar

Combine softened ice cream, macaroon crumbs, chopped almonds, and ½ cup Grand Marnier in a large mixing bowl; stir well. Freeze until firm.

Combine strawberries and sugar in a large saucepan. Cook over medium heat, stirring frequently, until sugar dissolves and strawberries are thoroughly heated.

Place remaining Grand Marnier in a small long-handled pan; heat just until warm. Pour over strawberries, and ignite with a long match. Baste strawberries with sauce until flames die down.

Place a scoop of prepared ice cream into individual serving bowls. Spoon strawberry mixture over each serving. Serve immediately. Yield: 24 servings.

Just ten cents for this 1894 Christmas issue of Ladies' Home Journal, featuring an elegant ball.

ADIES' HOME JOURNAL

Christmas
1894

ACKNOWLEDGMENTS

Amandine Chicken Sandwiches, Herbed Party Triangles, menu for "Morning Coffee in Atlanta" adapted from *Atlanta Cooks for Company* by The Junior Associates of the Atlanta Music Club, ©1968. By permission of The Junior Associates of the Atlanta Music Club, Georgia.

Anne's Pimiento Cheese Sandwiches, Wedding Punch courtesy of Mrs. L. J. Clark, Vicksburg, Mississippi.

Chatham Artillery Punch courtesy of Savannah Area Convention and Visitors Bureau, Savannah, Georgia.

Cheese Straws courtesy of Mrs. Mac Greer, Mobile, Alabama.

Chewy Blonde Brownies by Emma Stullken Webb, Elgin, Texas, first appeared in *Cook 'em Horns* by The Ex-Students' Association of the University of Texas, ©1981. By permission of The Ex-Students' Association, The University of Texas, Austin.

Chicken Croquettes, menu for "Atlanta Welcomes the Met" adapted from *Georgia Heritage: Treasured Recipes* by The National Society of the Colonial Dames of America in the State of Georgia, ©1979. By permission of The National Society of the Colonial Dames of America in the State of Georgia, Savannah.

Chicken Salad in Tart Shells, Cucumber Sandwiches, Fresh Fruit Salad with Celery Seed Dressing, Frozen Chocolate Dessert, Open-Face Date-Nut Sandwiches, Pineapple-Lemon Sherbet, Shrimp and Cream Cheese Triangles, Steamed Asparagus with Hollandaise Sauce adapted from *Gourmet of the Delta*, collected by St. John's Woman's Auxiliary and St. Paul's Woman's Auxiliary. By permission of St. John's Woman's Auxiliary, Leland, Mississippi.

Chicken with Sour Cream adapted from *Party Potpourri* by The Memphis Junior League, ©1971. By permission of The Memphis Junior League, Tennessee.

Chocolate-Mocha Cheesecakes by Elaine Martini Dove, Hamden, Connecticut, first appeared in *Cook 'em Horns* by The Ex-Students' Association of the University of Texas, ©1981. By permission of The Ex-Students' Association, The University of Texas, Austin.

Chutney Sandwiches, Wine Jelly with Sabayon Sauce adapted from *Harris County Heritage Society Cook Book* by William C. Griggs, ©1964. By permission of Harris County Heritage Society, Houston, Texas.

Congealed Tomato-Tuna Salad, Snowballs courtesy of Mrs. Glenn Scott, Garland, Texas.

Country Pâté, Sesame Chicken Wings, Sherried Pecans adapted from *Helen Exum's Cookbook* by Helen McDonald Exum, ©1982. By permission of Helen McDonald Exum, Chattanooga, Tennessee.

Cream of Broccoli Soup courtesy of Kaleen Berry, Birmingham, Alabama.

Deviled Ham Puffs adapted from *River Road Recipes* by The Junior League of Baton Rouge, ©1959. By permission of The Junior League of Baton Rouge, Inc., Louisiana.

Four O'clock Tea Scones adapted from *The Southern Cook Book* by Marion Brown, ©1968. By permission of The University of North Carolina Press, Chapel Hill.

Hot Chocolate, Refreshing Lemonade, Stuffed Yellow Squash adapted from *The Nashville Cookbook: Specialties of the Cumberland Region* by The Nashville Area Home Economics Association, ©1977. By permission of The Nashville Area Home Economics Association, Tennessee.

Hot Pepper Pecans by Twyla Lynn Tranfaglia, El Paso, Texas, first appeared in *Cook 'em Horns* by The Ex-Students' Association of the University of Texas, ©1981. By permission of The Ex-Students' Association, The University of Texas, Austin.

Kraut Balls courtesy of Mrs. Glenn McCluen, Knoxville, Tennessee.

Menu for "Cocktail Buffet at the First White House," menu for "Garden Tea at Magnolia Grove," Stuffed Breasts of Chicken adapted from *The Alabama Heritage Cook Book* by Katherine Durham and Susan Rush, ©1984. Courtesy of the authors and Heritage Publications, Birmingham, Alabama.

Menu for "Annapolis Ring Dance Banquet" adapted from *Brigade, Seats! The Naval Academy Cookbook* by Karen Jensen Neeb, ©1984. By permission of Glasgow Co., Ltd., Publishers, Washington, D.C.

Menu for "Polk Pilgrimage Luncheon" adapted from *The James K. Polk Cookbook* by The James K. Polk Memorial Auxiliary, ©1978. By permission of The James K. Polk Memorial Auxiliary, Columbia, Tennessee.

Miniature Biscuits adapted from *The Fredericksburg Home Kitchen Cookbook* by the Fredericksburg Parent-Teacher Association. By permission of The Fredericksburg Home Kitchen Cookbook Central Committee, Texas.

Mint Tea Punch by Sammie Farrier Marshall, Temple, Texas, first appeared in *Cook 'em Horns* by The Ex-Students' Association of the University of Texas, ©1981. By permission of The Ex-Students' Association, The University of Texas, Austin.

Mocha Milk Punch, Pineapple-Rum Bits adapted from *Le Bon Temps* by the Young Women's Christian Organization, ©1982. By permission of the Young Women's Christian Organization, Baton Rouge, Louisiana.

Onion Salad Dressing courtesy of Mrs. Guy Taliaferro, Sheffield, Alabama.

Orange Charlotte adapted from *Belle Meade Mansion Cookbook*. By permission of Belle Meade Mansion, Nashville, Tennessee.

Orange Ice adapted from *Atlanta Woman's Club Cookbook*, edited by the Home Economics Department, ©1921. By permission of the Atlanta Woman's Club, Georgia.

Pastel Cream Wafers courtesy of Emma Dean Tull, Pineville, Louisiana.

Sand Tarts adapted from *Little Rock Cooks* by The Junior League of Little Rock, ©1972. By permission of The Junior League of Little Rock, Inc., Arkansas.

Southern Baked Beans courtesy of Mrs. Carlyle Jennings, Murfreesboro, Tennessee.

Spinach Puffs adapted from *It's Greek to Me!* by the Philoptochos Society of Annunciation Greek Orthodox Church, ©1981. By permission of the Philoptochos Society of Annunciation Greek Orthodox Church, Memphis, Tennessee.

Spinach Soufflé with Mushroom Sauce, Stuffed Pork Tenderloins adapted from *The James River Plantations Cookbook* by Payne B. Tyler. By permission of The Williamsburg Publishing Co., Williamsburg, Virginia.

Steamboat Round of Beef courtesy of Mr. Nathan Madison, Chef, Ensley Grill, Ensley, Alabama.

Vegetable Sandwiches courtesy of Mrs. George W. Riddle, Gadsden, Alabama.

Back cover art from the Collection of Bonnie Slotnick.

INDEX